Great Vegan BBQ
WITHOUT A GRILL

Great Vegan BBQ
WITHOUT A GRILL

★ ★ ★ ≡ ✕ ≡ ★ ★ ★

★ ★ ★

Amazing Plant-Based Ribs, Burgers, Steaks,
Kabobs and More Smoky Favorites

★ ★ ★

★ **LINDA & ALEX MEYER** ★
The Mother-Daughter Team Behind Veganosity

PAGE STREET
PUBLISHING CO.

PAGE STREET
PUBLISHING CO.

THIS BOOK IS DEDICATED TO OUR READERS: Without your support, Veganosity and this cookbook wouldn't exist.

TO OUR FAMILY AND FRIENDS: Your never-ending support and cheerleading makes this journey of ours all the sweeter.

TO ALL OF THE ANIMALS THAT INSPIRE AND MOTIVATE US TO PROMOTE A VEGAN LIFESTYLE: May you one day live without fear.

CONTENTS

Introduction

We started our vegan journey just over three years ago. In that time, we created our blog, Veganosity, and began reinventing recipes that we grew up loving—the ones that reminded us of family. We could have said goodbye to them, as they were made with dairy and meat, but the idea of tossing aside traditions and memories seemed wrong and unnecessary. So, we dug in our heels, did our research and started coming up with ways to make plant-based versions of the foods that told our stories, such as pulled BBQ, spicy black bean burgers, macaroni and cheese, creamy potato salad, classic ribz, jerk chik'n and brisket.

The recipes in this book celebrate who we are, where we come from and our love of family, sports, the South, the Midwest and most of all, animals. Every one of our recipes has a story behind it. The BBQ recipes were inspired by family road trips from the Midwest to the Carolinas and every stop in between. Others were adapted from our favorite game day foods and weekends spent grilling in the backyard. And what we're most proud of is that every single recipe tastes like the ones we used to eat before going vegan.

Why BBQ that you can make in your kitchen, instead of on an outdoor grill? Because we live in the Midwest, and it's cold for nine months of the year! We learned many years ago that if we wanted BBQ in the middle of January, or even March, we could step outside and shiver while we cooked, or we could make it in the cozy warmth of our kitchen. That was a no-brainer. We also wanted to create recipes that you can make anywhere. If you live in an apartment and don't have access to a grill, no worries, you can still get your BBQ on. Granted, our BBQ isn't slow cooked in a hot smoker, but hey, veggies don't need hours to cook.

If you're looking for a healthier way to make BBQ and grilled foods, if you're wanting to add more plants to your diet, and if you're an animal lover like we are, then you've come to the right place. You're going to find more than 75 plant-based recipes that you can whip up for your next BBQ, tailgate or just because you're in the mood for a big ol' BBQ sandwich with a side of potato salad. We've created meaty recipes, burgers, side dishes, dips and an assortment of homemade BBQ sauces that you can add to almost anything.

Cooking healthy, plant-based, whole foods is our passion. We're home cooks who have decades of experience, and we love to get in the kitchen and play around with flavors. Creating recipes is like a science experiment. You add a little of this, a little of that, and you keep adding until you get it just right. Sometimes you win, and other times you fail. Oddly enough, it's the failures that keep us going, because those mistakes force us to keep trying until our recipes are just right. We're nothing if not tenacious, which is why we're confident that you're going to enjoy our recipes as much as we do. We shy away from bland and embrace bold flavors, we love a variety of textures in our food, and our mantra is "eat the rainbow." The more color you put in your diet, the happier and healthier you're going to be.

You're going to find that many of the recipes in this book are made with cauliflower, mushrooms, tofu, a variety of beans, jackfruit, cashews and vital wheat gluten. These seven ingredients are versatile, and are the perfect meat and dairy substitutes. Cauliflower is incredibly healthy, its texture is quite meaty when cooked properly and its somewhat non-existent flavor allows sauces and spices to take center stage. Mushrooms have a terrific meaty texture and a wonderful umami flavor.

Tofu is one of our favorite proteins, and, like cauliflower, it soaks up whatever flavor you marinate it in. Speaking of tofu, it really does get an undeserved bad rap. It's an excellent source of iron, amino acids, calcium and other nutrients. If you look at cultures that consume a lot of tofu, you'll find that they tend to be much healthier than those who eat a lot of processed foods that contain soy isolate, the not so healthy family member of the soy family. In this book, we prefer extra-firm tofu. The firmer the better.

Beans are magical, in the best way. They're little bombs of protein that will help you serve up delicious veggie burgers any day of the week. Jackfruit is another magical ingredient. It's a nutrition-packed fruit that's grown in Asia and tastes like bubble gum before it's cooked, but once you simmer it, shred it and smother it in your favorite BBQ sauce, you'll swear you're eating pulled pork or chicken.

Cashews are our best friend. When you soak them and grind them up in a blender or food processor, they get nice and creamy, and mimic anything, from a cream sauce to cream cheese. The best! We also used vital wheat gluten (VWG) to make our seitan ribz and brisket recipes. VWG is basically the protein from the endosperm of a wheat berry. It contains 70 to 80 percent protein. When it's mixed with liquid it turns into a stretchy dough, and when it's baked and then grilled, it takes on a tender, chewy texture that's similar to meat. Cool, right? Bob's Red Mill makes it and you can find it in Whole Foods and other specialty stores.

We're so grateful to have the opportunity to share our love of BBQ, grilling and vegan food with you, and we hope this cookbook will inspire you to get into your kitchen and make delicious vegan BBQ for you and your loved ones.

Linda & Ay

NOTES ON INGREDIENTS AND TOOLS

While most of the ingredients you'll find in the recipes in this cookbook are easy to find in your local supermarket, a few of them are not, such as jackfruit and vital wheat gluten (VWG). If you can't find one or both of these in your area, you can order them online.

JACKFRUIT

Jackfruit is a wonderful substitute for making pulled BBQ, chicken or crab dips, tacos and so much more. You can use fresh jackfruit if you wish, but it takes a lot of work to harvest the edible part from the fruit, and then you have to simmer it in liquid and bake it, plus, it's hard to find in many areas. We like to use prepared, canned young jackfruit packed in water; it's just easier. Our favorite is Native Forest brand. You can find it online or in your local Asian market.

VITAL WHEAT GLUTEN

This ingredient is a must for making vegan ribz, brisket, chik'n and other meaty recipes. We like Bob's Red Mill brand. You can purchase it online or at Whole Foods, specialty supermarkets and in the natural foods section in many chain grocery stores where they sell Bob's Red Mill products.

You can purchase prepared seitan, but if you want the best results for our ribz and brisket recipes, make it fresh.

AQUAFABA

Aquafaba is the juice, or brine, in canned beans. It's a fabulous binding agent that we love to use to keep veggie and bean burgers together, and it's also great for baking and making meringues. The brine from a can of chickpeas is the most preferred, but you can use the juice from any canned bean. You can also use the liquid from fresh beans if you prefer to soak and boil your own chickpeas. Store leftover aquafaba in the refrigerator in a sterile container with an airtight lid for up to 2 days, or in the freezer in an ice cube tray so you have measurable 1 tablespoon (15 ml) servings for up to a month.

LIQUID SMOKE

Liquid smoke can be found in the condiments aisle of most supermarkets. We use this in many of our BBQ recipes because it mimics the smoky flavor that comes from slow grilling. If you prefer not to use it, you can add smoked paprika, although this will alter the flavor profile. You could also omit it if you're grilling on an outdoor grill, but again, the intended flavor of the recipe won't be exactly the same.

NUTRITIONAL YEAST

Nutritional yeast is a vegan's best friend. It has a wonderful cheese-like flavor, and it's the perfect ingredient for anything that requires a cheesy taste. It's also a great source of vitamin B-12 and other nutrients. You can sprinkle it on almost anything. Note that this is not the same as Brewer's yeast or rising yeast. You cannot substitute either one of those yeasts for nutritional yeast.

PANS

The beauty of the recipes in this book is that you don't need to step outside to cook, although you're certainly welcome to use an outdoor grill. If you have an indoor grill or a grill pan, use it. Your burgers and ribz will get the same beautiful seared grill marks that they would on an outdoor grill. If you don't have either one of those, you can use a cast-iron skillet (our preferred pan), a standard skillet or a griddle.

CHAPTER 1

Meat-Free BBQ to Satisfy Meat Eaters

Never in a million years did we think that we'd be able to eat food like you'll find in this chapter. I stopped eating beef and pork in my twenties, and Alex never ate it. There were plenty of times throughout the past thirty something years that I wanted to dig into a pulled pork sandwich, dripping with BBQ sauce, but I never did. That's why this chapter is one of my favorites. The recipes are recreations of the food of my childhood. They're a combination of my mother's Southern roots and my father's love of ribs and grilled sausage. The best part? All of them can be made in your kitchen. No outdoor grill required.

These recipes were the most challenging and the most fun to develop, because they forced us to go deep into the creative process. You'll be amazed by how close they mimic the taste and texture of meat. The Classic BBQ Short Ribz (page 29) are perfectly chewy and drenched with tangy BBQ sauce, and the Old Bay Grilled Scallops (page 37) will make you think you're eating the real thing. You'll also love our Honey BBQ Ribz (page 18), South Carolina Pulled BBQ (page 22) and Texas BBQ Brisket (page 26). Satisfy those meat cravings, from chicken to steak, without the guilt. And make sure you have plenty of napkins on hand, because BBQ is messy business.

Many of the recipes in this chapter use vital wheat gluten and jackfruit; if you haven't read through the introduction yet, see page 13 to learn more about these ingredients.

Pulled New Orleans BBQ Seitan

The dark beer and the portobello mushrooms in this seitan recipe give it a nice umami flavor that even the most stubborn meat eater will like, and the hot and buttery New Orleans style BBQ sauce elevates it to another level of BBQ bliss. Top it with our Carolina Coleslaw (page 121).

SERVES 6

2 tsp (10 ml) extra-virgin olive oil, divided

1 cup (86 g) finely chopped portobello mushrooms

2 cups (240 g) vital wheat gluten

2 tsp (5 g) garlic powder

2 tsp (5 g) paprika

1 tsp smoked paprika

1 tsp ground annatto

1 tsp onion powder

1 tsp ground sea salt

½ cup (120 ml) dark beer

½ cup (120 ml) water

¼ cup (60 ml) low sodium soy sauce

1 tbsp (15 ml) vegan Worcestershire sauce

1 tbsp (15 ml) hickory-flavored liquid smoke

1 tbsp (15 g) tomato paste

2 tbsp (30 g) creamy peanut butter

SAUCE

3 tbsp (45 ml) vegan butter

3 cloves garlic, minced

¼ cup (60 ml) hot sauce

¼ cup (60 ml) vegan Worcestershire sauce

½ cup (120 ml) white wine

Juice of ½ lemon

¼ tsp black pepper

¼ tsp white pepper

¼ tsp chili powder

⅛ tsp cumin

½ tsp onion powder

⅛ tsp cayenne pepper

6 hamburger buns

Carolina Coleslaw (page 121)

Parsley sprigs (optional)

Preheat the oven to 350°F (176°C) and lightly grease a 9 × 9-inch (23 × 23-cm) pan.

Heat 1 teaspoon of oil in a skillet on medium-high heat. Add the mushrooms and cook for 5 to 7 minutes, until they're soft. Puree in a food processor or high-powered blender.

Whisk the vital wheat gluten, garlic powder, paprika, smoked paprika, annatto, onion powder and sea salt until fully combined.

In a separate bowl, whisk the beer, water, soy sauce, Worcestershire sauce, liquid smoke, tomato paste and peanut butter for approximately 1 minute. Combine with the dry mixture, add the mushrooms and stir until combined. Spread the dough evenly throughout the pan and press it into the corners. Bake for 40 minutes.

Heat a grill pan or skillet on medium-high heat and brush the seitan with the remaining teaspoon of oil. Sear the seitan 4 to 5 minutes per side, or until browned. Shred to look like pulled meat.

Melt the butter in a saucepan on medium heat. Add the garlic and brown for about 3 minutes. Add the hot sauce, Worcestershire sauce, white wine, lemon juice, black and white pepper, chili powder, cumin, onion powder and cayenne to the butter and garlic and stir. Add the shredded seitan and simmer for 15 minutes.

Pile on a hamburger bun and top with the slaw and a few sprigs of parsley for a burst of fresh flavor.

Honey BBQ Ribz

Ribs were one of my dad's favorite things to grill on a summer Sunday afternoon, so when
I realized that I could have that traditional food back in my life, it felt good. If he were still here,
I know he'd give these vegan ribz two thumbs up. The sauce is tangy, slightly sweet and savory,
and you don't need to cook it before slathering it on the ribz.

SERVES 4

3 tsp (20 ml) extra-virgin olive oil,
divided

2 cups (160 g) quartered white
mushroom caps

2 cups (240 g) vital wheat gluten

2 tsp (5 g) onion powder

1 tsp garlic powder

1 tsp smoked paprika

1 tsp sea salt

½ tsp black pepper

1 cup (240 ml) mushroom broth (we
use Pacifica brand)

¼ cup (60 ml) low sodium soy sauce

3 tbsp (45 g) peanut butter or any nut
butter, including tahini

2 tbsp (30 ml) hickory-flavored liquid
smoke

2 tbsp (30 ml) vegan Worcestershire
sauce (we use Annie's brand)

2 tbsp (30 g) tomato paste

1 tbsp (15 g) roasted beet or beet
juice (for color, optional)

½ cup (120 ml) ketchup

1 tbsp (15 ml) Dijon mustard

2 tbsp (30 ml) vegan honey (we like
Bee Free Honee)

2 tsp (10 ml) apple cider vinegar

1 tbsp (20 g) chili powder

1 tsp cumin

¼ tsp ground sea salt

¼ tsp ground black pepper

Preheat the oven to 350°F (176°C) and grease a 9 × 9-inch (23 × 23-cm) pan.

In a medium skillet, heat 2 teaspoons (10 ml) of olive oil on medium-high heat. Add the mushrooms and cook until soft, approximately 5 minutes, then set aside.

In a large bowl, whisk the gluten, onion powder, garlic powder, paprika, salt and pepper until well combined.

In a food processor or high-powered blender, add the cooked mushrooms, broth, soy sauce, peanut butter, liquid smoke, Worcestershire sauce, tomato paste and beet until pureed, approximately 1 minute. Pour the mushroom mixture into the gluten mixture and stir until it turns into a light and bubbly dough. Spread it evenly in the greased pan and bake for 30 minutes.

Mix the ketchup, mustard, honey, vinegar, chili powder, cumin, salt and pepper in a small bowl to make the sauce. Slather the sauce on both sides of the ribz.

Heat a grill pan or skillet on medium-high heat and brush with the remaining teaspoon of olive oil. Grill the ribz for approximately 3 to 4 minutes or until you see grill marks. Slice into strips and enjoy!

BBQ Jackfruit with Grilled Pineapple

★ ★ ★ ≡ ✕ ≡ ★ ★ ★

This is one of our go-to recipes because it's so easy and quick to make. Even though there are only five ingredients, the sweet caramelized pineapple and the hot and spicy chipotle BBQ sauce make it taste like there's a lot going on. You get a bit of sizzle and sweet in every delicious bite. This is a favorite among our friends and family. Pair this with our Spicy Grilled Corn on the Cob (page 118) and Mom's Creamy Cucumber Salad (page 122) for a down home kind of supper.

SERVES 4

2 (14-oz [400-g]) cans young jackfruit, drained and rinsed

4 cups (960 ml) vegetable broth

1 small pineapple

1 tbsp (15 ml) vegetable oil

2 cups (480 ml) Have-It-Your-Way Chipotle BBQ Sauce (page 162) or store-bought sauce

4 hamburger buns

Shredded green or red cabbage

In a medium saucepan, bring the broth to a boil and reduce to a low simmer. Add the jackfruit to the broth and simmer for 20 minutes.

While the jackfruit is simmering in the broth, slice 3 round ½-inch (13-mm)-thick pieces of pineapple and remove the skin. Brush the oil on the grill pan or skillet and heat it on medium heat. When the pan is hot, add the pineapple and grill for approximately 3 to 4 minutes per side, or until it's nicely seared and you can see caramelized grill marks. Then, coarsely chop the pineapple.

When the jackfruit is finished simmering, drain the broth and shred the jackfruit with a fork or pulse in a food processor about six to ten times. It should resemble pulled meat.

Bring the BBQ sauce to a boil in a saucepan over medium-high heat and add the jackfruit and pineapple. Stir to combine and reduce the heat to a low simmer. Cook for 20 minutes, stirring frequently.

Put the BBQ jackfruit on the hamburger bun and top with the shredded cabbage.

South Carolina Pulled BBQ

★ ★ ★ ✖ ★ ★ ★

South Carolina and its mustard BBQ sauce will forever have a piece of my heart. My childhood family vacations to Myrtle Beach meant numerous stops at BBQ shacks, and this tangy sauce has always been one of my favorites. When I took the first bite of our vegan version I was stunned by how much it tasted like the sandwiches I remembered. Jackfruit is magical. When pulled, it truly replicates the texture of meat. Simmering it in the no-chicken broth makes shredding it easier and gives the fruit a mild and savory flavor. The mustard sauce is a departure from the red sauces that most people are used to. It has a tangy vinegar flavor that's a fun change of pace from typically sweet BBQ sauce. You can make it and eat it immediately, but if you want the flavor to really develop, refrigerate it overnight.

SERVES 4

1 cup (240 ml) yellow mustard

¼ cup (60 ml) apple cider vinegar

½ cup (120 ml) white wine vinegar

3 tbsp (42 g) packed brown sugar

1 tbsp (15 ml) vegan Worcestershire sauce (we use Annie's brand)

3 tsp (15 ml) extra-virgin olive oil, divided

½ tsp garlic powder

½ tsp ground sea salt

1 tsp hot sauce (optional)

2 (14-oz [400-g]) cans young jackfruit

24 oz (720 ml) no-chicken broth

1 yellow onion, thinly sliced

4 hamburger buns (optional)

Shredded cabbage

Whisk the mustard, vinegars, brown sugar, Worcestershire sauce, 2 teaspoons (10 ml) of olive oil, garlic powder, sea salt and hot sauce in a saucepan until well combined. Bring to a boil and then reduce the heat and simmer for approximately 20 minutes, or until it thickens, stirring frequently. For best results, pour into a glass jar, cover with a lid and refrigerate overnight. This allows the flavors to mingle and intensify.

Drain and rinse the jackfruit well. Put the jackfruit and the broth in a large saucepan and stir to combine. Bring to a boil, then reduce and simmer for 1 hour. Drain the excess broth and shred the jackfruit. It should resemble pulled meat.

Heat 1 teaspoon of olive oil in a large skillet on medium-high heat. Add the onions and the jackfruit and cook until the onions are soft and the jackfruit begins to brown, approximately 8 minutes. Add 3 tablespoons (45 ml) of the BBQ sauce and stir until it's fully incorporated into the jackfruit. Serve it on a bun or eat it plain, just make sure you spoon extra sauce on top. Add shredded cabbage for a fresh crunch.

Chipotle BBQ Grilled Cauliflower Steaks with Chimichurri

Meaty, charred to perfection and satisfying is how we describe our cauliflower steaks. Cauliflower is such an underrated vegetable, and we're on a mission to change that. Not only is it one of the healthiest vegetables, it's a fabulous meat substitute because of its chewy texture. Cauliflower soaks up the flavor that it's marinated in, and our chipotle BBQ sauce gives the steaks a sweet and spicy flavor that's so delicious paired with our bright and fresh chimichurri sauce. You can grill the steaks or roast them in your oven. Serve them with our Southern-Style Skillet Cornbread (page 129) and Smoky Skillet BBQ Baked Beans (page 138).

SERVES 4

1 large cauliflower head

1 cup (240 ml) Have-It-Your-Way Chipotle BBQ Sauce (page 162) or your favorite store-bought sauce

1 tbsp (15 ml) extra-virgin olive oil

Ground sea salt and black pepper to taste

1 cup (240 ml) 10-Minute Homemade Chimichurri (page 173)

Remove the leaves from the cauliflower and place it stem side up on a cutting board. Slice through center of the stem. Cut 2 steaks ½ inch (1.3 cm) thick from one of the cauliflower halves. Repeat with the other half. You should get 4 steaks plus smaller florets, which can be grilled with the steaks.

Fill a stock pot with water and bring it to a boil, add the cauliflower steaks and florets and cook for approximately 10 minutes, or until they're fork tender. Remove, place on a plate lined with paper towels and pat dry.

Pour the BBQ sauce in a large baking dish and put the cauliflower steaks in the pan. Turn them over several times and dip the edges so the sauce covers the steaks. Marinate for 10 minutes then flip and marinate the other side for 10 minutes.

TO GRILL

Heat the grill pan on medium-high heat and brush with the oil. When the pan is hot put the cauliflower steaks on, and salt and pepper to taste. Cook for approximately 5 minutes per side (brush any leftover BBQ sauce on the steaks every time you flip them) or until the steaks have grill marks. Lower the temperature to medium-low and cook for approximately 10 minutes per side or until the steaks are caramelized and tender.

TO ROAST

Preheat the oven to 375°F (191°C) and coat a rimmed baking sheet with the oil. Roast the cauliflower for 10 to 12 minutes per side, or until the edges are golden brown. Brush with any excess BBQ sauce when you flip them.

To serve, spoon a liberal dollop of the chimichurri sauce on top.

Texas BBQ Brisket

★ ★ ★ ≡ ✕ ≡ ★ ★ ★

This vegan brisket is about as close as you're going to get to the real thing. It took us at least seven tries to get this brisket just right. The key to our success was adding finely shredded jackfruit, dark beer and red miso paste. The jackfruit nailed the texture we were looking for, and the beer and miso gave it a rich umami flavor. We love this with our Mom's Creamy Cucumber Salad (page 122) and Smoky Skillet BBQ Baked Beans (page 138).

SERVES 4 TO 6

1 (14-oz [400-g]) can young jackfruit

2 cups (240 g) vital wheat gluten

3 tbsp (30 g) nutritional yeast

1 tbsp (7 g) smoked paprika

1 tsp garlic powder

1 tsp onion powder

1 tsp annatto

3 tsp (15 g) coarsely ground sea salt, divided

1½ cups (360 ml) dark beer

2 tbsp (30 g) red miso paste

1 tbsp (15 ml) soy sauce

2 tbsp (30 ml) vegan Worcestershire sauce (we use Annie's brand)

2 tbsp (32 g) cashew butter

3 tbsp (45 ml) liquid smoke

3 tbsp (45 ml) extra-virgin olive oil, divided

1 small roasted beet, pureed (for color, optional)

1 tbsp (15 g) coarsely ground pepper

1 tsp paprika

1 tsp chili powder

½ tsp granulated sugar

½ cup (120 ml) Big Mama's Homemade BBQ Sauce (page 161) or store bought (optional)

Preheat the oven to 350°F (176°C).

Drain and rinse the jackfruit. Pulse it in a food processor until shredded, approximately ten to fifteen pulses.

In a large bowl, whisk the gluten, nutritional yeast, paprika, garlic powder, onion powder, annatto and 1 teaspoon of salt until fully combined.

In another large bowl, whisk the beer, miso paste, soy sauce, Worcestershire sauce, cashew butter, liquid smoke and 2 tablespoons (30 ml) of olive oil until combined.

Add the jackfruit, beet and the beer mixture to the gluten mixture and stir until it turns into a solid ball of stretchy dough. Don't overstir the dough or it will get tough. Place the dough on a lightly oiled baking sheet and form into the shape of a brisket, about 10 inches (25 cm) long and 1½ inches (4 cm) thick.

Whisk 2 teaspoons (10 g) of salt, black pepper, paprika, chili powder and sugar together until well combined. Evenly sprinkle the salt rub mixture over the top and gently rub it on the top of the brisket. Bake for 40 minutes.

If you like the brisket grilled with BBQ sauce, brush all sides with sauce and grill on medium-high heat in a grill pan or skillet. Cook for 3 to 4 minutes per side, or until it has grill marks.

Classic BBQ Short Ribz

There's nothing fancy about these classic ribz. They're tender, meaty, chewy and dripping in sweet and sticky sauce to satisfy you and whoever you're serving them to. Serve them up with our Spicy Sweet Potato Wedges (page 134) and our Grilled Wedge Salad with Vegan Ranch Dressing (page 133) for the perfect barbecue dinner.

SERVES 4 TO 6

3 tsp (15 ml) extra-virgin olive oil, divided

2 cups (154 g) coarsely chopped white mushroom caps

2 cups (240 g) vital wheat gluten

2 tsp (5 g) garlic powder

2 tsp (5 g) paprika

1 tsp smoked paprika

1 tsp ground annatto

1 tsp onion powder

1 tsp ground sea salt

1 cup (240 ml) mushroom broth, plus more if needed

½ cup (120 ml) dark beer

¼ cup (60 ml) soy sauce

1 tbsp (15 ml) vegan Worcestershire sauce (we use Annie's brand)

1 tbsp + 1 tsp (20 ml) hickory-flavored liquid smoke

1 tbsp (15 g) tomato paste

2 tbsp (32 g) natural creamy peanut butter

2 cups (480 ml) Big Mama's Homemade BBQ Sauce (page 161) or your favorite store bought sauce

Sliced jalapeño peppers

Minced cilantro

Heat 2 teaspoons (10 ml) of the olive oil in a medium skillet on medium-high heat. Add the mushrooms and cook until they're soft and browned, approximately 5 minutes. Let cool.

In a large bowl, whisk the gluten, garlic powder, paprika, smoked paprika, annatto, onion powder and salt until fully combined.

Preheat the oven to 375°F (191°C) and lightly oil a 9 × 9-inch (23 × 23-cm) square pan.

Put the mushrooms, broth, beer, soy sauce, Worcestershire sauce, liquid smoke, tomato paste and peanut butter in a food processor or a high-powered blender and blend for approximately 1 minute or until smooth and creamy. Pour it into the dry mixture and stir until it turns into a stretchy ball of dough. Knead for about 1 minute.

Pat the dough flat so it spreads evenly in the pan until it reaches all four corners. Bake for 30 minutes. Let cool for 10 to 15 minutes, then remove from the pan and cut in half lengthwise. Use a sharp knife and score (don't cut all the way through) the ribz horizontally, about 1 inch (25 mm) thick. Each half should look like a rack of ribs.

Heat a grill pan or skillet on medium-high heat and brush with 1 teaspoon of olive oil. Slather the sauce on all sides of the ribz and cook for 3 to 4 minutes per side, or until you see grill marks or a browned surface.

Use extra BBQ sauce for dipping. Serve with sliced jalapeño peppers and minced cilantro for extra flavor.

Beer Braised Pulled Pork

Simmering jackfruit in dark beer gives it a rich umami flavor that goes perfectly with the earthy and savory sauce. You can eat this alone, or stuff it on a bun. We love this paired with our Smoky Grilled Broccoli (page 125).

SERVES 4

3 tbsp (45 ml) balsamic vinegar

1 tbsp (15 ml) vegan Worcestershire sauce (we use Annie's Brand)

1 tbsp (15 g) tomato paste

¼ tsp maple syrup

½ tsp garlic powder

1 tsp chili powder

⅛ tsp cinnamon

2 (14-oz [400-g]) cans young jackfruit

2 tsp (10 ml) extra-virgin olive oil

1 small white onion, chopped

12 oz (354 ml) dark beer

3 cloves garlic

Salt and pepper to taste

4 hamburger buns

TOPPINGS

Sliced red onion

Arugula

In a medium bowl, whisk the balsamic vinegar, Worcestershire sauce, tomato paste, maple syrup, garlic powder, chili powder and cinnamon until fully combined to make the sauce.

Drain and rinse the jackfruit and coarsely chop until it resembles pulled meat. You could also use a food processor and pulse 6 to 8 times.

In a Dutch oven or a deep stock pot, heat the oil on medium heat. When the oil is hot, add the onion and cook, stirring frequently, until it becomes translucent, approximately 5 minutes. Pour the beer into the pot, add the garlic cloves and bring to a boil. Add the jackfruit and stir. Cook until the beer is reduced by two-thirds, approximately 10 minutes. Reduce the heat to a low simmer and let the remaining liquid cook until it's mostly evaporated, about 5 to 7 minutes, leaving approximately 3 tablespoons (45 ml). Add salt and pepper to taste, then add the sauce. Stir until the jackfruit is completely coated. Turn the heat to the lowest setting and let simmer for 20 minutes, stirring frequently. Remove the garlic cloves.

Serve on a bun with a topping of sliced red onion and peppery arugula.

Boneless BBQ Buffalo Wings

In Chicago, BBQ is synonymous with sporting events and therefore perpetually linked with wings. However, since going the veg-head route, we thought we had to abandon those tangy little treats. Not anymore! We've come up with a way to eat wings and save the chickens too. These go great with our Smoky Mac 'n' Cheese with Coconut Bacon (page 101).

MAKES APPROXIMATELY 20 WINGS

2 tbsp (14 g) ground flax seed

¼ cup (60 ml) water

10 oz (283 g) extra firm tofu, drained

1¼ cups (156 g) breadcrumbs

½ cup (120 ml) Have-It-Your-Way Chipotle BBQ Sauce (page 162) or store bought

1 tbsp (15 g) Bragg's Sprinkle Seasoning

½ tsp salt

1 cup (240 ml) Smoky, Buttery Buffalo Sauce (page 174)

Preheat the oven to 350°F (176°C).

Mix the ground flax and water in a small bowl and let it set for 10 minutes.

In a food processor, pulse the tofu, flax seed mixture, breadcrumbs, BBQ sauce, Sprinkle Seasoning and salt until a uniform blend is created.

Line a baking sheet with parchment paper. Form the tofu mixture into about twenty 2-inch (4-cm) wing/nugget shapes and place them on the baking sheet. Bake them for 30 minutes. Take them out of the oven, toss the wings in the buffalo sauce and serve hot.

Easy Meaty Portobello Steaks with Chimichurri

* * * ≡ ✕ ≡ ★ ★ ★

Even when I used to eat meat, I always thought that a grilled portobello cap tasted like steak. The rich, umami flavor of mushrooms, especially a portobello, seated next to a pile of spicy sweet potato wedges, is a vegan's version of a meat and potato kind of meal. This recipe will satisfy the veg-heads and the pickiest omnivore at your table, especially when you spoon a dollop of our homemade chimichurri sauce on top. If you need to make more than four steaks, just double up the recipe. It couldn't be easier.

SERVES 4

½ cup (120 ml) 10-Minute Homemade Chimichurri (page 173)

3 cloves garlic, minced

¼ cup (60 ml) teriyaki sauce

1 tbsp (15 ml) extra-virgin olive oil

½ tsp smoked paprika

½ tsp ground black pepper

½ tsp ground sea salt

4 large portobello mushroom caps, stems removed

4 servings Spicy Sweet Potato Wedges (page 134)

Make the chimichurri sauce and allow the flavors to infuse while you prepare the portobello steaks.

Whisk the garlic, teriyaki sauce, olive oil, paprika, pepper and salt together in a medium bowl until fully combined.

Place the mushroom caps on a large platter and brush the garlic mixture over both sides. Let sit for 20 minutes.

Heat a grill pan or a skillet on medium-high heat and grill the mushrooms for 10 to 12 minutes per side, or until they're slightly charred and are fork tender. Put a liberal dollop of chimichurri sauce over the steaks and serve with the Spicy Sweet Potato Wedges.

Old Bay Grilled Scallops

When I went vegan, the two foods that I really missed were pulled BBQ and grilled scallops. It took me a while to find a good plant-based substitute for the scallops, but when I finally did, all felt right with the world. White mushroom caps are like sponges. If you soak them overnight in a broth with Old Bay seasoning, they become spongy in texture and soak up the seasoning, which always reminds me of grilled scallops. The truth is, scallops don't really have a flavor if they're fresh, that's why the ones that I had at the beach always had some Old Bay sprinkled on them. Thankfully, mushrooms come so close to tasting like scallops when they're prepared this way that if I close my eyes and take a bite, I feel like I'm on the South Carolina coast, with a slight sunburn and a plate of my favorite seafood. You'll want to make our Carolina Coleslaw (page 121) and Cheesy Grits (page 130) to pair with these.

SERVES 4

24 oz (679 g) white mushroom caps

32 oz (946 ml) mushroom broth (we use Pacifica brand)

2 tbsp (12 g) Old Bay seasoning

2 tsp (10 ml) extra-virgin olive oil, divided

Salt and pepper to taste

Slice a thin layer off of the top of the mushroom heads and then slice the stems off. They should have a flat top, like a scallop.

Whisk the broth, seasoning, 1 teaspoon of olive oil, salt and pepper in a large bowl and add the mushrooms. Cover and refrigerate overnight.

Heat a grill pan or a skillet on medium-high heat and brush with the remaining olive oil. Drain the mushrooms, and when the pan is hot, cook them for approximately 8 minutes per side, or until they're golden brown.

Pulled Shiitake Mushroom BBQ

★ ★ ★ ≡ ✗ ≡ ★ ★ ★

This is for our mushroom lovers. If that's you, and you love a meaty and chewy pulled BBQ sandwich, then you're going to want to pull out your pan and start making this ASAP! Dripping in thick BBQ sauce and topped with arugula, tomato and pickle slices is how we like to eat this delightfully satisfying sandwich. One of the most popular recipes on our blog is our Pulled BBQ Carrots. They have a nice meaty texture that mimics pulled pork, and they're delicious. Because we're always trying to improve every recipe we make, we experimented with a lot of different vegetables to come up with a meatier and chewier pulled BBQ that's just as easy to whip up for a crowd. The clear winner was this recipe. We combined shiitake and portobello mushrooms because together they are an excellent meat substitute, and because two mushroom flavors are better than one. This sandwich pairs nicely with our Spicy Sweet Potato Wedges (page 134).

SERVES 4

2 cups (480 ml) Big Mama's Homemade BBQ Sauce (page 161) or store bought

22 oz (624 g) shiitake mushrooms

22 oz (624 g) baby portobello mushrooms

1 tbsp (15 ml) extra-virgin olive oil

1 large white or yellow onion, finely diced

Salt and pepper to taste

4 hamburger buns

TOPPINGS

Arugula

Tomato slices

Sliced dill pickles

Make the BBQ sauce, if you don't already have some on hand, to allow the flavors to infuse while you prepare the mushrooms.

Thinly slice the mushrooms. They should look shredded. Heat the oil in a large skillet on medium heat. Depending on the size of the pan, you may need to cook the mushrooms and onions in two batches. When the oil is hot, add the mushrooms and onions and stir frequently until the mushrooms lose their water and the onions become translucent and soft, approximately 5 to 7 minutes.

Turn up the heat to medium-high and add salt and pepper to taste. Cook until the onions caramelize and the edges of the mushrooms begin to crisp up, approximately 5 minutes.

When the mushrooms and onions are done cooking, add the BBQ sauce to the pan and stir until the mushrooms are completely coated in the sauce. Bring the mixture to a boil on medium heat and then reduce the heat to a low simmer. Cook for 15 minutes, stirring frequently, until the sauce is thick and sticky.

Serve the mushrooms on the buns and top with the arugula, tomato and sliced pickles.

Gluten-Free Grilled Eggplant Sausage

★ ★ ★ ═ ⚔ ═ ★ ★ ★

This recipe is for those of you who can't, or won't, eat gluten, and would love to sink your teeth into a BBQ sausage. Most store-bought vegan sausages have vital wheat gluten as a main ingredient, so those won't work for you. Thankfully, that's about to change.

We came up with this idea while testing an eggplant steak recipe. We thought, why not slice them into spears, instead of discs, and marinate them in the herbs and spices that you'd find in sausage? We did that, then grilled them in our kitchen, stuck them in a roll and topped them with caramelized onions, vegan ricotta and balsamic vinegar. One bite in and we knew we had a winner. If you don't need the recipe to be gluten-free, you can use regular wheat sausage rolls. We love these with our Smoky Skillet BBQ Baked Beans (page 138).

SERVES 4 TO 6

¼ cup + 1 tsp (65 ml) avocado or olive oil, divided

1 small red onion, thinly sliced

1 tbsp (2 g) dried Italian seasoning

1 tsp ground sea salt

⅛ tsp ground white pepper

⅛ tsp ground celery seed

1 tbsp (15 ml) lemon juice

1 large eggplant

Gluten-free sausage/hot dog rolls

TOPPINGS

Caramelized onions

Vegan ricotta

Balsamic vinegar

Arugula or lettuce

Heat 1 teaspoon of oil in a skillet on medium heat. When the oil is hot, add the onions and stir. Cook until they lose their water and caramelize, stirring frequently, approximately 5 to 7 minutes.

Meanwhile, whisk ¼ cup (60 ml) of oil, Italian seasoning, salt, white pepper, celery seed and lemon juice until fully combined.

Cut the stem and the end off of the eggplant and peel. Slice in half lengthwise and then cut each half in half. If the eggplant is really fat, keep going. Each sausage should be about 1½ inches (3.8 cm) thick. Put the eggplant spears in a shallow dish and pour the oil mixture on top and toss and rub it in to fully coat. Don't let the oil sit on the eggplant too long or it will get soggy.

Heat a grill pan or skillet on medium-high heat. When the grill is hot put the eggplant on and cook for approximately 3 minutes per side, or until all sides are nicely browned and have grill marks. The eggplant should be fork tender.

Tuck the sausages into the rolls, top with the onions, vegan ricotta and greens, and drizzle with balsamic vinegar.

BBQ Jerk Chik'n

★ ★ ★ ⚌ ✕ ⚌ ★ ★ ★

If you love jerk chicken, and you love BBQ chicken, you're going to fall head over heels for our BBQ Jerk Chik'n. We took the spicy flavor of the Caribbean and the sweet BBQ sauce of the South and combined them to give you the best of both worlds. You're going to get hot and savory flavors from the jerk rub and brown sugar and spice from the BBQ sauce in every bite of our seitan chik'n strips. This has turned into one of our favorite grilling foods. Serve as an entrée, or slice into strips and put them over salads, or in a wrap. You could pair it with our Grilled Wedge Salad with Vegan Ranch Dressing (page 133) to make a hearty meal.

SERVES 4 TO 6

1 tbsp (15 ml) vegan chicken bouillon (we use Better Than Bouillon brand)

2 cups (480 ml) boiling water

2 cups (240 g) vital wheat gluten

1 cup (160 g) brown rice flour

1 tbsp (10 g) nutritional yeast

½ tsp ground sea salt

3 tbsp (19 g) Homemade Jerk Rub (page 178) or store bought

1 cup (240 ml) Big Mama's Homemade BBQ Sauce (page 161) or your favorite store-bought sauce

1 tsp extra-virgin olive oil

Dissolve the bouillon in the water and whisk until fully combined.

In a large bowl, whisk the gluten, rice flour, yeast and salt until fully combined. Add 1 cup (240 ml) of the broth and stir. Slowly add more broth as needed until it turns into a stretchy ball of dough. Knead the dough for 2 minutes and roll it into a log.

Place a steamer basket in a large stockpot and fill with water, just under the top of the basket. You don't want water to touch the seitan dough. Add any remaining broth to the water. Bring to a boil and place the seitan on the basket. Reduce the heat to a simmer, cover and steam for 30 minutes.

Remove the seitan from the basket and place on a parchment-lined baking sheet. Refrigerate for 2 hours.

Spread the jerk rub evenly on a flat plate. Slice the chik'n loaf into ½-inch (13-mm)-thick pieces and dip all sides in the rub.

Heat a grill pan or skillet on medium-high heat and brush the oil on the pan. When it's hot (the chik'n pieces should sizzle when they touch the pan), place the chik'n pieces on the pan and brush the tops with a thick layer of BBQ sauce. Cook for 2 minutes and flip. Brush the upright side with a thick layer of sauce and cook for another 2 minutes. Flip one more time and cook for 1 minute.

Spicy Grilled Crab Patties with Aioli

✦ ✦ ✦ ═ ⚔ ═ ✦ ✦ ✦

Shredded artichokes with a little bit of seaweed are dead ringers for crab. We've served these delicious cakes to numerous friends who were blown away to learn that what they were eating was not crab. These are so easy to make, and you can freeze them if you want to make them ahead of time. Make large crab cakes for a meal, or make little appetizer-size cakes for a party. And definitely dip them in our Vegan Aioli (page 170). Pair it with our Mom's Creamy Cucumber Salad (page 122) and Spicy Grilled Corn on the Cob (page 118).

MAKES 6 TO 8 PATTIES

2 tbsp (14 g) ground flaxseed

¼ cup (60 ml) water

2 (12-oz [340-g]) cans quartered artichokes hearts, in water

¼ cup (3 g) seaweed snacks (we use Annie Chun's Organic Roasted Sea Salt)

1 jalapeño pepper, minced

¼ cup (44 g) minced red bell pepper

¼ cup (25 g) chopped green onions

1 tbsp (15 ml) hot sauce

1 tsp horseradish mustard

2 tsp (10 g) Old Bay Seasoning

1 tsp garlic powder

Sea salt to taste

1½ cups (188 g) panko breadcrumbs

2 tsp (10 ml) olive oil

SERVE WITH

Cocktail sauce

Vegan Aioli (page 170) or vegan ranch dressing

Lemon wedges

In a small bowl, whisk the flaxseed and water until it forms a sticky paste. Set aside.

Drain the artichokes and rinse them well. Now, pulse the seaweed snacks in a food processor until they look like small flakes. Remove them from the food processor and place in a large bowl. Place half the artichokes in a food processor and blend until smooth and creamy, put them in the bowl with the seaweed flakes. Put the other half of the artichokes in the food processor and pulse ten times, or until they break up into small chunks. Add to the bowl with the pureed artichokes and seaweed flakes.

Mix the artichokes together in a large bowl with the flax mixture, jalapeño, bell pepper, green onion, hot sauce, horseradish mustard, old bay seasoning, garlic powder and salt. Add the breadcrumbs and mix until well combined.

Form the mixture into ½-cup (116-g) patties.

Heat a grill pan or skillet on medium-high heat. Brush the cakes on both sides with the olive oil. Grill the cakes for approximately 3 to 4 minutes per side, or until grill marks appear and they're golden brown. Serve with cocktail sauce, aioli and lemon wedges.

CHAPTER 2

Burgers and Sandwiches: From Way Up North to the ★ Deep South ★

Smoky, sizzling, sweet or boot kickin' spicy, you'll find your favorite burger or sandwich in this tasty chapter. The burgers are made with everything from black beans and black-eyed peas to lentils, so there's a burger for everyone, and all of them are filled with spice and topped with one of our delectable BBQ sauces or creamy toppings. We've created Smoky Chipotle BBQ Black Bean Burgers (page 49), Sizzling Mushroom Burgers (page 50), Sweet Little Chickpea Sliders (page 53) and Boot Kickin' BBQ Cauliflower Tacos (page 77), plus many more mouthwatering recipes that require a bun, tortilla or even a lettuce wrap, if you're watching your carbs.

Every one of the recipes was tested and approved by some of the most discerning foodies we know. We suggest that you begin with the Grilled Confetti Veggie Burgers with Chimichurri (page 70). They got rave reviews from all who tried them.

FYI, most of the burgers call for aquafaba. This is the liquid in which beans have been cooked, or the juice that's in a can of beans. It's a fantastic binding agent that will ensure that your burgers won't fall apart. You can read more about aquafaba on page 13.

Smoky Chipotle BBQ Black Bean Burger

⋆ ⋆ ⋆ ≡ 🍴 ≡ ⋆ ⋆ ⋆

This mouthwatering black bean burger gets two thumbs up from our family and friends every time we serve it. It has so much BBQ flavor, it's hearty and satisfying, and you don't have to grill it on an outdoor grill to get a nice smoky flavor. Besides the taste, you're also going to love how crispy the exterior gets when you brush on the sticky BBQ sauce and then sear it. These burgers stay together, thanks to aquafaba, so feel free to grill them on an outdoor grill as well. Serve them with our Southern-Style Creamy Potato Salad (page 117) and Collard Greens with a Kick (page 137) for a homegrown kind of meal.

SERVES 6

½ cup (120 ml) Have-It-Your-Way Chipotle BBQ sauce (page 162), divided

3 tsp (15 ml) extra-virgin olive, divided

1 small white onion, finely diced

3 tbsp (32 g) seeded, chopped poblano pepper

2 (15-oz [425-g]) cans black beans, divided (reserve liquid)

½ cup (86 g) yellow cornmeal

½ cup (45 g) oat flour

3 tbsp (45 ml) aquafaba

1 tsp salt

Pepper to taste

6 hamburger buns

TOPPINGS

Lettuce

Vegan cheese

Vegan Buttermilk Ranch Dressing (page 166) or store bought

Make the Have-It-Your-Way Chipotle BBQ Sauce (page 162) if you don't already have some on hand.

Heat 1 teaspoon of olive oil in a medium skillet on medium heat. Add the onion and poblano pepper and cook, stirring frequently, until the onion is soft and translucent, approximately 5 minutes.

Drain the beans (reserve the liquid) and rinse well. Put 2¼ cups (140 g) of the beans in a food processor and pulse until they're creamy. Scrape the beans into a mixing bowl and add the remaining whole beans. Add the onion and peppers, cornmeal, oat flour, aquafaba, 3 tablespoons (45 ml) of BBQ sauce, salt and pepper to the bowl and stir until combined.

Scoop a ½ cup (120 ml) of the black bean mixture from the bowl and form into a patty. Continue making patties with the rest of the mixture. Brush a liberal layer of the BBQ sauce on both sides of the burgers.

Heat a grill pan or a skillet on medium-high heat and brush with 2 teaspoons (10 ml) of oil. Place the burgers in the pan, cover and cook for approximately 5 to 7 minutes, gently flip and cook for another 5 to 7 minutes. Even though these burgers hold together well, they're still veggie burgers, and can break apart if you are too rough while flipping.

Put the lettuce on the buns and top with the vegan cheese and ranch dressing.

Sizzling Mushroom Burgers with Horseradish Pesto

★ ★ ★ ═ ✕ ═ ★ ★ ★

Mushrooms' chewiness and umami flavor make them a great choice for a veggie burger. This mushroom burger recipe is made with white button mushrooms, pecans and quinoa, which adds protein and lends a wonderful crunchy texture. They also have a slight kick to them, thanks to the chipotle chili powder. We topped these with our Horseradish Pesto (page 169) for a touch of heat. Serve them with our Roasted Lemon Dill Asparagus (page 126) and Southern Boil Grill Packets (page 105) for the perfect meal.

SERVES 6

½ cup (86 g) dry quinoa

1 cup (240 ml) water

8 oz (227 g) white button mushrooms, stems removed

2 tbsp (15 ml) extra-virgin olive oil

1 cup (110 g) toasted pecan chips

1 large shallot, finely chopped

2 cloves garlic, minced

1 cup (90 g) oat flour

1 tsp ground cumin

½ tsp chipotle chili powder

1 tsp ground sea salt

Black pepper to taste

1 tsp liquid smoke (optional)

3 tbsp (45 ml) aquafaba

1 tbsp (15 ml) vegetable oil

6 hamburger buns

TOPPINGS

Horseradish Pesto (page 169)

Lettuce or spinach

Shredded cucumber

Rinse the quinoa in a fine mesh strainer for 2 minutes to remove its bitter saponin coating. In a small saucepan, combine the water and quinoa and bring to a boil. Reduce the heat to a low simmer, cover and cook for approximately 15 minutes or until the water evaporates. Remove from the heat and let it sit while you prepare the rest of the ingredients.

For best results, finely chop the mushrooms in a food processor, or chop by hand. Heat the oil in a medium skillet on medium heat. When the oil is hot, add the mushrooms, pecans, shallot and garlic. Stir to combine and cook for approximately 5 minutes, or until the mushrooms have cooked off their water.

While the mushrooms and quinoa are cooking, whisk the oat flour, cumin, chili powder, salt and black pepper together in a large mixing bowl. Add the mushroom mixture, quinoa (make sure the quinoa is dry and fluffy, not wet), liquid smoke and aquafaba, and stir until completely combined and sticky. Form the mixture into 6 round patties.

Heat a grill pan or skillet on medium heat and brush a layer of oil on top. When the pan is hot, cook the mushroom patties for approximately 8 to 10 minutes per side (covered), or until they're nicely seared and heated through.

Top with the Horseradish Pesto, lettuce or spinach, and shredded cucumber.

Sweet Little Chickpea Sliders

These adorable little sliders pack a punch of flavor, especially after you slather on a schmear of our Avocado Lime Sauce (page 177). They're the perfect party food, or you can make larger patties for a small gathering. We love to serve these with a big batch of our Spicy Sweet Potato Wedges (page 134).

MAKES APPROXIMATELY 12 SLIDERS

2 (15-oz [425-g]) cans chickpeas/
garbanzo beans

2 tbsp (30 ml) extra-virgin olive oil,
divided

1 white onion, finely diced

1 orange bell pepper, stem and seeds
removed, finely diced

2 cloves garlic, minced

½ cup (20 g) fresh parsley, stems
removed

2 tbsp (30 ml) aquafaba (bean liquid,
see page 13)

1 cup (90 g) oat flour

1 tbsp (15 ml) lemon juice

2 tsp (5 g) ground cumin

2 tsp (5 g) Italian seasoning

Salt and pepper to taste

A dozen slider buns

TOPPINGS

Shredded cabbage

Tomato

Avocado Lime Sauce (page 177)

Drain the beans (reserve the aquafaba from the cans) and rinse well.

Heat 1 tablespoon (15 ml) of the oil in a medium skillet on medium heat. When the oil is hot add the onions and peppers. Cook for 5 minutes, stirring frequently. Add the garlic to the pan and stir. Cook for 1 minute, remove from the heat and let cool.

Process the garbanzo beans, parsley and 2 tablespoons (30 ml) of aquafaba in a food processor until the beans are mostly smooth and sticky. Transfer to a large mixing bowl and add the oat flour, sautéed onion and peppers, lemon juice, cumin, Italian seasoning, salt and pepper. Stir to fully combine. Scoop out 2 tablespoons (28 g) and form into a round patty. Continue the process until you've used up the mixture.

Heat a grill pan or skillet on medium heat and brush the remaining oil on the pan. When the oil is hot add the patties and cover. Cook for approximately 5 to 7 minutes per side, or until they have distinct grill marks and are golden brown.

Put the cabbage, tomato and Avocado Lime Sauce on the buns and top with the sliders.

Cheddar Stuffed Veggie Burgers

There is nothing like this burger, and I mean nothing. It literally has vegan cheddar cheese buried in the center. All it will take is one delicious bite of this savory veggie burger with the cheese slowly melting in your mouth, and you'll have to admit that you've fallen in love with a burger.

SERVES 4

1 large beet

1 tsp coconut oil

1 cup (120 g) all-purpose flour

½ cup (62 g) breadcrumbs

1 tsp salt

2 tbsp (30 g) Bragg's Sprinkle Seasoning (or a general poultry seasoning)

1 (15-oz [425-g]) can chickpeas

⅓ cup (80 ml) aquafaba

½ cup (62 g) shredded vegan cheddar cheese

1 tbsp (15 ml) olive oil

4 hamburger buns

TOPPINGS

Lettuce

Vegan Buttermilk Ranch Dressing (page 166)

Preheat the oven to 375°F (191°C).

Cover the beet in coconut oil and bake for 50 minutes. Remove the beet from the oven and allow it to cool.

While the beet is cooling, combine the flour, breadcrumbs, salt and Sprinkle Seasoning together and set aside. Once the beet is cooled, remove the skin and place the beet in a food processor with the chickpeas and aquafaba. Blend until smooth and creamy. Add the chickpea–beet mixture to the flour mixture and knead until well combined.

Form the mixture into thin patties about 5 inches (13 cm) in diameter. Pile about 2 tablespoons (15 g) of cheese on the center of half the patties. Top the cheese patties with a plain patty and press together to form a large, cheese-filled patty.

Heat the olive oil in a grill pan or skillet on medium-high heat and cook the patties (covered) for approximately 10 minutes per side.

Put the shredded lettuce on the buns and place the burgers on the lettuce, then top with the ranch dressing.

Chicago-Style Not Dogs

Chicago is known for deep-dish pizza and hot dogs. Hot dogs are taken seriously in Chi-Town, and there are some strict rules when it comes to what you put on a hot dog, and in what order. The hot dog always comes first when building a true Chicago dog, but since we don't partake in those anymore, we start with our carrot dogs. That's right, carrots. A parboiled carrot (shaved into the shape of a hot dog), marinated in spices and liquids that mimic the flavor of a hot dog. When tucked into a bun and topped with the necessary ingredients that make up a Chicago-style hot dog, you'll never know that they're made out of rabbit food. And, they're doggone delicious! Pair with our Spicy Sweet Potato Wedges (page 134) and Smoky Skillet BBQ Baked Beans (page 138).

SERVES 6

6 large carrots, peeled and ends cut or rounded off with a peeler

¼ cup (60 ml) white balsamic vinegar

2 tbsp (30 ml) vegan Worcestershire sauce (we use Annie's brand)

1 tbsp (15 ml) soy sauce

1 tsp yellow mustard

1 tsp smoked paprika

½ tsp liquid smoke

¼ tsp onion powder

¼ tsp ground sea salt

⅛ tsp garlic powder

⅛ tsp black pepper

1 tbsp (15 ml) extra-virgin olive oil

6 sesame seed buns

TOPPINGS

Yellow mustard

Relish

Chopped onion

Tomato slices

Pickle slices

Sport peppers (pickled jalapeños or pepperoncini will work too)

Celery salt

Bring a large pot of water to a boil. Add the carrots and cook for approximately 10 to 15 minutes, or until they're fork tender. They should be soft but not mushy. Remove from the water and put the carrots in a deep baking dish and score them with a knife, about 6 times across.

Whisk the vinegar, Worcestershire sauce, soy sauce, mustard, paprika, liquid smoke, onion powder, salt, garlic powder and black pepper until completely blended. Pour the sauce over the carrots and roll them so they're completely coated. Cover and refrigerate overnight so the sauce soaks in. Roll occasionally so all sides soak up the marinade.

After the carrots are finished marinating, take them out of the refrigerator and bring them to room temperature, approximately 30 minutes.

Oil a grill pan or skillet and heat on medium heat. Cook the carrots for about 4 to 5 minutes per side, or until they have dark grill marks or they're seared and are heated through to the center.

Put the carrots in the buns and top with the mustard, relish, onion, tomato, pickles, sport peppers and celery salt.

NOTE: For best results make the day before serving so the carrots can soak up the marinade.

★ ★ ★

Smoky Mountain Lentil Burgers

These smoky lentil burgers were inspired by the memory of driving through the Great Smoky Mountains in the back of our family's red station wagon on our way to Myrtle Beach, South Carolina. We always stopped at the same little truck stop to pick up burgers and fries just before we got to the mountains. They weren't made with lentils or beets, but they did have a fabulous smoky flavor from the grill. These burgers have the same smokiness; only they're so much better for you. These go great with our Spicy Grilled Corn on the Cob (page 118) and our Carolina Coleslaw (page 121).

SERVES 6

1 medium or 2 small red beets

1 cup (204 g) uncooked lentils

4 cups (1 L) water

1 cup (163 g) cooked brown rice

1 cup (90 g) oat flour

2 tsp (5 g) ground cumin

1 tsp smoked paprika

1 tsp ground sea salt

½ tsp chili powder

½ tsp liquid smoke

1 tsp vegan Worcestershire sauce

3 tbsp (45 ml) aquafaba

Black pepper to taste

1 tsp extra-virgin olive oil

6 hamburger buns

TOPPINGS

Shredded romaine lettuce

Tomato slices

Avocado slices

Vegan Aioli (page 170)

Preheat the oven to 400°F (204°C).

Wash and pat the beet dry, and roast for approximately 45 minutes or until the beet is fork tender. Let it cool, peel and puree the beet in a food processor.

In a fine mesh strainer, rinse the lentils. Put them in a large saucepan and cover with the water and bring to a boil. Reduce the heat to a simmer and partially cover with a lid to allow some of the steam to escape. Cook for 30 to 40 minutes or until the lentils are soft. Drain the excess water.

In a large mixing bowl, stir the beets, lentils, rice, oat flour, cumin, paprika, sea salt, chili powder, liquid smoke, Worcestershire sauce, aquafaba and black pepper, until fully combined. Form the mixture into 6 equal patties. Let the patties rest for 15 to 20 minutes.

Heat a grill pan or skillet on medium heat and brush the oil on the grill. When the pan is hot, put the burgers on and cover with a lid to ensure that they heat all of the way through. Cook for approximately 10 minutes then flip and cover again. Cook for another 10 minutes.

Put a pile of lettuce on the bun, top with the tomato, add the burger and put a few slices of avocado and a dollop of aioli on top.

Easy Peasy Black-Eyed Pea Burgers

★ ★ ★ ⫶ ✕ ⫶ ★ ★ ★

Black-eyed peas are not peas at all, they're beans, and they're full of calcium, folate, protein and fiber. No wonder they're thought to bring good luck if you eat them on New Year's Day! Because of the earthy flavor of black-eyed peas, we prefer making savory burgers out of them. When you mix them with onion, garlic, mushrooms, fresh sage and Italian seasoning, that earthiness turns into something otherworldly. They're so fragrant and delicious, I'm sure that our Southern grandmother would approve. We love these with our Collard Greens (page 137) and our Baby Potato Packets with Lemon and Dill (page 110).

SERVES 4 TO 6

1 (15-oz [425-g]) can black-eyed peas

2 tbsp (30 ml) extra-virgin olive oil, divided

1 small red onion, finely chopped

1 small carrot, finely chopped

1 cup (75 g) chopped mushrooms

1 tsp chopped fresh sage

1 tbsp (8 g) dried Italian seasoning

2 large cloves garlic, minced

½ cup (66 g) oat flour

1 cup (112 g) panko breadcrumbs

¼ cup (60 ml) aquafaba

Salt and pepper to taste

4 to 6 hamburger buns

TOPPINGS

Sliced red onion

Lettuce

Horseradish Pesto (page 169)

Drain (reserve ¼ cup [60 ml] of the liquid) and rinse the black-eyed peas. Pulse them in a food processor, approximately eight to ten pulses, or in a high-powered blender until they're almost smooth and creamy yet retaining some pieces of the beans.

Heat 1 tablespoon (15 ml) of olive oil in a large skillet on medium heat. When the oil is hot, add the onion, carrots and mushrooms and cook, stirring frequently, until the mushrooms are soft and browned, approximately 5 to 7 minutes. Add the sage, Italian seasoning and garlic and cook for 2 minutes, stirring well.

Put the black-eyed peas, oat flour, breadcrumbs, cooked vegetables, reserved aquafaba, salt and pepper in a large mixing bowl and stir until combined and sticky. Divide into 4 to 6 equal parts and form into patties.

Heat a grill pan or skillet on medium-high heat and brush with the remaining oil. Place the patties on the grill and cover. Cook approximately 10 minutes per side, or until they're golden brown and have distinct grill marks.

Top with sliced red onion, lettuce and Horseradish Pesto.

Home on the Range Buffalo Quinoa Burgers

★ ★ ★ ═ ✕ ═ ★ ★ ★

When people typically think of vegans, we're guessing that two foods usually pop into their heads: kale and quinoa. And yes, while this recipe does have quinoa, we're not ashamed of using this vegan-stereotype . . . why? Because quinoa makes bomb buffalo quinoa burgers! It perfectly absorbs the buffalo sauce, allowing it to create a buffalo flavor explosion on your tongue with every bite. You're welcome. For a well-balanced meal, pair this with our Grilled Potato Steaks (page 95) and Smoky Grilled Broccoli (page 125).

SERVES 4

1 medium sweet potato

2 tsp (10 ml) olive oil, divided

2½ cups (462 g) cooked quinoa

2 tbsp (14 g) ground flax seed

¼ cup (60 ml) water

⅓ cup (80 ml) Smoky, Buttery Buffalo Sauce (page 174)

1 tsp garlic powder

¼ tsp ground black pepper

½ tsp salt

1 cup (120 g) breadcrumbs

4 pretzel buns

TOPPINGS

Arugula

Tomato slices

Cucumber slices

Vegan Buttermilk Ranch Dressing (page 166)

Preheat the oven to 400°F (204°C).

Pierce the sweet potato ten times and brush with 1 teaspoon of olive oil. Bake the sweet potato on a baking sheet in the oven for 1 hour.

Remove the sweet potato from the oven and let cool. Once the sweet potato is cool, remove the skin and mash the sweet potato in a large mixing bowl with the quinoa until uniform in appearance.

Combine the flax and water in a small bowl and let it sit for 2 minutes.

Mix the buffalo sauce, flax mixture, garlic powder, black pepper and salt with the sweet potato mixture and breadcrumbs and form into 4 large patties.

Preheat a grill pan or skillet on medium-high heat and brush with the remaining 1 teaspoon of olive oil. Cover and sear the quinoa burgers for approximately 8 minutes per side.

Top with the arugula, tomato, cucumber and ranch dressing.

Take Me to Texas Southwestern Burgers

★ ★ ★ 〓 ✕ 〓 ★ ★ ★

Before Alex was born, my husband and I used to fly to Dallas when we needed to get away from the Chicago winter. We loved the city, the weather and the food. I can't remember the name of the restaurant that we used to go to for lunch, but they had an incredible black bean burger that I absolutely pined for when we were back in the Midwest. That burger had all of the flavors of one perfectly spicy taco, and I'm a big fan of tacos. The savory spices, jalapeño, black beans and garlic were reminiscent of my favorite veggie tacos, and that's why I had to replicate that burger for this cookbook. I hope you enjoy it as much as I do. This is so good with our Carolina Coleslaw (page 121) and Southern-Style Creamy Potato Salad (page 117).

SERVES 6

5 tsp (25 ml) extra-virgin olive oil, divided

1 red onion, finely diced

1 large or 2 small jalapeño peppers, seeded and finely diced

1 red bell pepper, seeded and finely diced

2 cloves garlic, minced

2 (15-oz [425-g]) cans black beans

1 cup (90 g) oat flour

2 tsp (5 g) ground cumin

1 tsp chipotle chili powder

1 tsp smoked paprika

1 tsp ground sea salt

Black pepper to taste

2 tbsp (30 ml) aquafaba

6 hamburger buns

TOPPINGS

Romaine lettuce

Tomato slices

Sliced red onion

Avocado slices

Heat 2 teaspoons (10 ml) of the oil in a large grill pan or skillet on medium heat. Add the onion, jalapeño and bell pepper and stir evenly throughout the pan. Cook for 4 minutes, stirring frequently. Add the garlic, stir to combine and cook for 1 minute. Let cool.

Drain the beans (reserve the liquid) and rinse well. Put the beans in a food processor and pulse until the beans are mostly creamy, approximately fifteen to twenty pulses. Scrape the beans into a mixing bowl and add the onion and pepper mixture, oat flour, cumin, chili powder, smoked paprika, salt, black pepper and aquafaba, stir until completely combined and sticky. Divide the mixture into 6 parts, roll into balls and form into patties.

Heat a grill pan or skillet on medium-high heat and brush with olive oil. Add the burgers, cover and cook for approximately 10 minutes per side, or until they're heated through and are golden brown with grill marks. Put the burgers on the buns and add the lettuce, tomato, sliced onion and avocado on top of the burger.

Wisconsin-Style Grilled Bratwurst

★ ★ ★ ≡ ✕ ≡ ★ ★ ★

My father's (Alex's grandfather's) favorite grilling food was bratwurst. In honor of him, I've created a vegan version of the classic Wisconsin bratwurst. Brats are meant to go with our Smoky Skillet BBQ Baked Beans (page 138) and Southern-Style Creamy Potato Salad (page 117).

SERVES 6 TO 8

3 tbsp (45 ml) extra-virgin olive oil, divided

1 medium eggplant, peeled and coarsely chopped

1 white or yellow onion, coarsely chopped

2 cloves garlic, minced

1 cup (120 g) garbanzo bean flour

2 cups (240 g) vital wheat gluten

1 tsp onion powder

1 tsp garlic powder

1 tbsp (8 g) dried Italian seasoning

1 tsp celery salt

1 tsp ground sea salt

½ tsp ground black pepper

½ cup (120 ml) beer

½ cup (120 ml) vegetable broth

¼ cup (60 ml) soy sauce

2 tbsp (30 ml) vegan Worcestershire sauce (we use Annie's brand)

1 tbsp (15 ml) extra-virgin olive oil

Hot dog buns

TOPPINGS

Mustard

Sauerkraut

In a large skillet, heat 1 tablespoon (15 ml) of olive oil on medium heat. Add the eggplant and onion. Stir and cook for 5 minutes. Reduce the heat to medium-low and cook for 10 minutes, stirring frequently. Add the garlic and cook for 1 minute. Remove from the heat and let cool.

In a large bowl, whisk together the bean flour, gluten, onion powder, garlic powder, Italian seasoning, celery salt, salt and pepper until combined.

In a small bowl, whisk together the beer, broth, soy sauce and Worcestershire sauce until combined. Pour into the dry mixture. Add the eggplant and onion and stir until the mixture turns into a stretchy dough. Add more gluten if needed. Knead the dough for 2 minutes then scoop out ¼ cup (61 g) of the dough and roll into a cylinder, approximately 4 inches (10 cm) long. Roll each sausage up tightly in a 12 × 12-inch (30 × 30-cm) piece of aluminum foil and twist the ends shut.

Bring a large pot of water to a boil and drop the sausages into the pot and boil for 45 minutes. Remove the sausages from the pot of water and put on a plate to cool. Refrigerate for at least 2 hours.

Bring the sausages to room temperature and remove the foil before grilling.

Heat a grill pan or skillet on medium-high heat and add the remaining olive oil. Cook the brats for 2 to 3 minutes per side, or until golden brown.

Serve in the buns topped with mustard and sauerkraut.

Pulled Sweet Potatoes with Have-It-Your-Way Chipotle BBQ Sauce

✦ ✦ ✦ ≡ ⚔ ≡ ✦ ✦ ✦

Pulled BBQ is done in so many different ways in the South. Every state seems to have its own way of making it. In the vegan world, we need to have several options too, because not everyone likes every vegetable. So this is for those of you who may not like pulled mushroom BBQ, or can't get their hands on jackfruit. We believe in equal opportunity. This sweet potato recipe is a twist on our Pulled Carrots BBQ, one of the most popular on our blog. Sweet potatoes offer a sweeter flavor and a slightly different texture than carrots. Many of our readers asked us to create a sweet potato version, so this is for them.

The key to preventing the potatoes from having a mushy texture is to finely shred them, and then roast them until they begin to dry out and the edges get crispy and brown. We coat them in our fiery Have-It-Your-Way Chipotle BBQ Sauce (page 162), which complements the sugary potatoes. We love these with our Spicy Grilled Corn on the Cob (page 118) and Collard Greens with a Kick (page 137).

SERVES 4

2 large sweet potatoes

1 large red onion, thinly sliced

1 tbsp (15 ml) extra-virgin olive oil

Salt and pepper to taste

2 cups (480 ml) Have-It-Your-Way Chipotle BBQ Sauce (page 162)

4 hamburger buns

TOPPINGS

Thinly shredded red cabbage

Sweet pickle slices

Preheat the oven to 375°F (191°C) and line a rimmed baking sheet with parchment paper.

Peel and finely shred the potatoes with a food processor or a box grater and spread them out evenly on the baking sheet. Sprinkle the onions over the top of the potatoes and drizzle with the olive oil. Salt and pepper to taste and toss the potatoes and onion. Bake for approximately 15 minutes, or until the edges of the potatoes begin to brown. Remove from the oven and put the potatoes and onions in a medium saucepan with the BBQ sauce and heat on medium heat for 10 minutes.

Pile the BBQ sweet potatoes on the buns and top with the cabbage and pickle slices.

Grilled Confetti Veggie Burgers with Chimichurri

★ ★ ★ ≡ ✕ ≡ ★ ★ ★

These fun and vibrant burgers were inspired by our love of Lilly Pulitzer. Her clothes are the epitome of bright, wild, bold and colorful, like confetti. Southern women love Lilly and color and weekend barbecues, just like we do, so we designed a burger around all of those things. Enjoy these with our Smoky Grilled Broccoli (page 125) and Mom's Creamy Cucumber Salad (page 122).

SERVES 4 TO 6

⅓ cup (80 ml) 10-Minute Homemade Chimichurri (page 173)

3 green onions, trimmed and cut in half

1 cup (130 g) coarsely chopped carrots

1 red bell pepper, seeded and cut into 4 large pieces

2 tsp (10 ml) extra-virgin olive oil, divided

2 (15-oz [425-g]) cans great northern white beans

2 to 3 tbsp (30 to 45 ml) aquafaba

1 cup (66 g) panko breadcrumbs

1 tbsp (6 g) chili powder

1 tsp cumin

½ tsp dried oregano

½ tsp garlic powder

½ tsp onion powder

1 tsp ground sea salt

Black pepper to taste

4 to 6 hamburger buns (optional)

TOPPINGS

Spinach or lettuce leaves

Smoky Blackened Corn Salsa (page 149)

10-Minute Homemade Chimichurri (page 173)

Make the chimichurri if you don't already have some on hand.

Place the green onions, carrots and bell pepper in a food processor and pulse until the vegetables are ground into small pieces. If you don't have a processor, finely chop them.

Heat 1 teaspoon of the olive oil in a medium skillet over medium heat. Scrape the vegetables into the pan and stir so they're evenly distributed. Cook 5 to 7 minutes, stirring often until the vegetables are soft. Let cool.

Drain the beans, reserving the aquafaba. Place one can of beans in a food processor or high-powered blender and pulse until the beans are creamy. Scrape the beans into a large bowl.

Pulse the second can of beans until the beans are partially blended. You should be able to see whole pieces of the beans. Scrape the beans into the bowl with the first can of beans. Add the breadcrumbs, sautéed vegetables, 2 to 3 tablespoons (30 to 45 ml) of the reserved aquafaba and the chili powder, cumin, oregano, garlic powder, onion powder, salt and pepper to the bowl and stir until combined. Divide by 4 or 6 and form the mixture into patties.

Heat a grill pan or skillet on medium-high heat. Brush it with the remaining oil, put the patties on the pan and cover. Cook until the bottoms are seared and have dark grill marks. Flip the burgers and sear the other side. Reduce heat to medium-low and cook for 10 minutes per side.

Serve on hamburger buns with spinach or lettuce, corn salsa and chimichurri sauce, or just wrap in lettuce for a low-carb option.

NOLA Grilled Beef Po' Boys

When we think of Louisiana, we think of New Orleans, and when we think of NOLA, we think of po' boys. Roast beef with gravy is a popular version of this classic sandwich, and we've veganized it so we and our veggie friends can enjoy one too. Grilled portobello mushrooms add a delicious smoky flavor, and they're so meaty and chewy even meat eaters will enjoy this recipe. All you'll need on the side of one of these delicious sandwiches is a pile of our Collard Greens (page 173).

SERVES 4

4 cloves garlic crushed and coarsely chopped

2 cups (480 ml) mushroom broth

1 tbsp (15 ml) vegan Worcestershire sauce (we use Annie's brand)

1 tbsp (15 ml) balsamic vinegar or red wine

2 tsp (5 g) Italian seasoning

Salt and pepper to taste

2 tbsp (30 ml) extra-virgin olive oil

12 large portobello mushrooms, washed, patted dry, stems removed

1 tbsp (10 g) cornstarch

¼ cup (60 ml) water

4 sandwich-size baguettes

TOPPINGS

Vegan mayonnaise or our Vegan Aioli (page 170)

Vegan mozzarella (we like Miyoko's Kitchen brand)

Shredded red cabbage or lettuce

Sliced tomatoes

Thin pickle slices

Place the garlic and the broth in a medium saucepan on medium heat and bring to a boil. Stir the Worcestershire sauce, vinegar, Italian seasoning, salt and pepper into the broth until combined and reduce the heat to low. Let simmer, stirring frequently, while you grill the mushrooms.

Heat a grill pan or a large skillet on medium-high heat. Brush the mushrooms with the olive oil, salt and pepper to taste. When the pan is hot, place the mushrooms top side up and cook for 6 to 8 minutes or until the mushrooms are nicely browned. Flip and cook for another 6 to 8 minutes.

While the mushrooms are cooking, whisk the cornstarch and water together and slowly pour it into the broth while whisking constantly. Whisk until the broth thickens and becomes a gravy. Continue to simmer and stir frequently.

Remove the mushrooms from the grill/pan and thinly slice. Put them in the pan with the gravy and stir well. Simmer for 15 minutes and add salt and pepper to taste.

Slice the rolls in half lengthwise, then scoop out the bread in the center. Spread a layer of mayonnaise or aioli on the rolls, pile the mushrooms on the bread and top with the mozzarella, shredded cabbage or lettuce, tomatoes and pickle slices. Dip in any leftover gravy.

TIP: If you want melty mozzarella, put it under the broiler for a few minutes.

★ ★ ★

Kentucky Bourbon BBQ Quesadillas

★ ★ ★ 〓 ✕ 〓 ★ ★ ★

These quesadillas are a delicious combination of Tex-Mex and Southern BBQ. Our Spicy Grilled Corn on the Cob (page 118) is the perfect side for these. For best results, start the cashew cheese the day before.

SERVES 4 TO 6

FOR THE CASHEW CHEESE

1 cup (113 g) raw cashews

3 tbsp (45 ml) lemon juice

2 cloves garlic

½ tsp smoked paprika

1 tbsp (12 g) nutritional yeast

¼ tsp ground sea salt

½ cup (120 ml) hot water

FOR THE QUESADILLAS

1 (14-oz [400-g]) block super firm tofu

⅓ cup (83 ml) Big Mama's Homemade BBQ Sauce (page 161), plus extra for drizzling

3 tsp (9 g) coconut sugar or brown sugar

1 cup (240 ml) bourbon

1 medium red bell pepper, thinly sliced

1 medium green bell pepper, thinly sliced

1 medium onion, thinly sliced

2 tsp (10 ml) extra-virgin olive oil

Salt and pepper to taste

12 (6-inch [15-cm]) or 8 (8-inch [20-cm]) flour tortillas

Cilantro, for topping

Cover the raw cashews in hot water for 3 hours. For best results soak overnight in the refrigerator. Drain and rinse.

Place the cashews, lemon juice, garlic, smoked paprika, nutritional yeast, salt and water in the blender and blend on a high speed until smooth and creamy. The cheese should be slightly thin but not runny. Set aside.

Press the liquid out of the tofu, approximately 10 minutes. Crumble the tofu into a small bowl with the BBQ sauce, toss until coated and set aside in the refrigerator.

In a small saucepan on medium heat, whisk the sugar and the bourbon until the sugar is dissolved and it begins to boil. Reduce the heat to low and stir constantly until it's reduced to a thick and sticky marinade, approximately 10 minutes.

Toss the peppers and onions in the bourbon–sugar mixture until well coated. Cover and refrigerate for at least 2 hours.

Heat the oil in a large pan on medium-high heat. Sauté the bell pepper–onion mixture and stir frequently until the onions become translucent. Reduce heat to medium-low and cook, stirring often, until the onions caramelize, approximately 8 to 10 minutes.

Add the tofu to the bell pepper–onion mixture, add salt and pepper to taste and stir for approximately 1 to 2 minutes. Remove from the heat.

Spread 1 tablespoon (15 ml) of cashew cheese on top of a tortilla, then a layer of the bell pepper–onion mixture on top of the cheese. Drizzle another tablespoon (15 ml) of cashew cheese on top of the veggies and put a tortilla on top. Repeat with the remaining ingredients.

Heat a grill pan or skillet on medium heat and brush with the oil. Cook the quesadillas for approximately 4 to 5 minutes per side or until golden brown (flip carefully).

Let the quesadillas rest for 4 to 5 minutes, then slice into quarters. Drizzle with any extra BBQ sauce you have left and sprinkle with cilantro.

Boot Kickin' BBQ Cauliflower Tacos with Avocado Lime Sauce

We eat tacos at least twice a week, and one of our favorites is spicy BBQ cauliflower tacos. When you boil the cauliflower, then smother it in the sauce and roast it, the texture becomes firm, yet chewy. It's not hard, it's not soft, it's just perfect. Boiling the cauliflower softens it, which allows the cauliflower to soak up the BBQ sauce, so you get a kick of spicy in every single bite.

SERVES 4 TO 6

1 head cauliflower

2 cups (480 ml) Have-It-Your-Way Chipotle BBQ Sauce (page 162) or store bought

6 flour or corn tortillas

TOPPINGS

Vegan refried beans (most brands are vegan)

Shredded red cabbage

Diced tomatoes

Salsa

Avocado slices

Vegan cheese

Preheat the oven to 375°F (191°C).

Remove the leaves from the cauliflower and slice in half down the center of the stem. Slice each half into steaks about 1 inch (25 mm) thick. Repeat on the other half.

Bring a large pot of water to a boil. Add the cauliflower steaks and any extra florets you may have. Boil for 10 minutes or until you can easily pierce the cauliflower with a fork. They should be tender, but not falling apart soft. Drain and place in a shallow baking dish.

Coat the cauliflower in the BBQ sauce and roast for approximately 25 minutes, or until the cauliflower is slightly charred and the sauce is dark and caramelized.

Heat the tortillas and fill with the refried beans, cauliflower, cabbage, tomatoes, salsa, avocado slices and vegan cheese.

Alabama White Sauce BBQ Sloppy Joes

★ ★ ★ 〓 ✕ 〓 ★ ★ ★

Where are our mayonnaise lovers? If that's you, then you're going to love this recipe. It was inspired by the classic sloppy joe, and our desire to create one more dish with our Sweet Home Alabama White BBQ Sauce. This Northern Alabama sauce is traditionally made with mayo, but we used cashews to create the creamy texture, which also adds protein to the mix. We made the sloppy joes with crumbled cauliflower, white mushrooms, onion, garlic and spices. It has just the right amount of savory and tangy. Make this simple, easy and delicious twist for your next tailgate party. Your guests will devour it. Serve this with our Spicy Sweet Potato Wedges (page 134).

SERVES 4

1 large cauliflower head

1 tbsp (15 ml) extra-virgin olive oil

3 cups (230 g) chopped white mushrooms

1 white onion, finely diced

1 tsp ground cumin

1 tsp chili powder

½ tsp white pepper

Salt to taste

2 cloves garlic, minced

1 cup (240 ml) Sweet Home Alabama White BBQ Sauce (page 162)

4 hamburger buns or mini baguettes

Cilantro

Sliced jalapeño peppers

Remove the core from the cauliflower and finely chop into pebble-sized pieces.

Heat the oil in a large skillet on medium-high heat. When the oil is hot, add the cauliflower and cook for 10 minutes. Add the mushrooms, onions, cumin, chili powder, pepper and salt and stir to combine. Cook for 15 minutes, stirring frequently. Add the garlic and cook for 2 minutes. Add the BBQ sauce and stir to combine. Cook for approximately 5 minutes, or until the sauce is hot.

Serve on buns with cilantro and sliced jalapeño peppers. Drizzle extra sauce over the tops if desired.

Loaded Grilled Veggie Sandwich with Horseradish Pesto

★ ★ ★ ═ ✗ ═ ★ ★ ★

On a warm summer day, there is nothing we love better than a fresh loaded veggie sandwich. Crunchy bread, warm grilled vegetables and a fresh and spicy pesto take a typical veggie sandwich to a whole new level. You can mix things up and use whatever vegetables you have on hand, or whatever is in season. We love using eggplant, zucchini and red peppers because they're readily available, no matter what time of year.

SERVES 4

1 small eggplant

1 large zucchini

1 red bell pepper

1 tbsp (15 ml) extra-virgin olive oil

1 tsp liquid smoke

1 clove garlic, minced

½ tsp black pepper

½ tsp salt

1 large baguette, sliced into 4 pieces and cut lengthwise

¼ cup (60 g) Horseradish Pesto (page 169), plus more for topping

1 large avocado, sliced

1 cup (20 g) fresh basil

1 cup (20 g) arugula

Vegan mozzarella (optional)

Slice the eggplant, zucchini and bell pepper lengthwise and about ½ inch (13 mm) thick to fit the length of the pieces of bread.

In a small bowl, whisk the olive oil, liquid smoke, garlic, black pepper and salt together until well combined.

Heat up a grill pan or skillet on medium-high heat. Brush the olive oil mixture onto each side of the eggplant, zucchini, pepper and the interior sections of the bread. Place the eggplant, zucchini and bell peppers on the pan, and cook on each side for approximately 8 to 10 minutes, or until fork tender and browned. Remove from the pan.

Grill the bread for about 1 to 2 minutes per side, or until golden brown. Spread the Horseradish Pesto on the bread and top with the vegetables, avocado, basil and arugula. Add vegan mozzarella if desired.

CHAPTER 3

Stick Food: Because Eating Food Off a Stick Is Fun!

How many of you remember eating food off a stick as a kid and loving it? We call it carnival food, because when you're walking around and eating, food is easier to eat when it's attached to a stick. As the refined adults we now are, we call stick food kabobs, but let's not be refined. Let's go back to our carefree days as kids and grill up some tasty food on sticks, because you only live once.

These special recipes are all near and dear to our hearts. You'll love our Spicy BBQ Bean Balls (page 89). They're just like the little appetizers you find at holiday parties. And our Smoky Tofu Bacon and Pineapple Kabobs (page 85) were a huge hit with our testers. Go ahead and make them all and invite your friends over to reminisce about your childhoods and enjoy food on a stick.

Smoky Tofu Bacon and Pineapple Kabobs

★ ★ ★ 🍴 ✕ 🍴 ★ ★ ★

We love tofu for many reasons, and we especially love that it absorbs the flavors of whatever you marinate it in. That's why it's one of our favorite ingredients for making "bacon." Before I became a vegetarian, one of my favorite appetizers was bacon and pineapple bites. My mouth would start watering the minute I heard them start to sizzle on the grill. Fortunately, you don't need a grill to make these sweet and savory kabobs. You can use your oven to get the same results, so you can enjoy them at any time of year. Make long skewers for a meal, or short picks for appetizers. They're wonderful on their own or on a bed of Cheesy Grits (page 130) for a quick and easy dinner.

SERVES 4

14 oz (397 g) extra-firm tofu

¼ cup (60 ml) low-sodium soy sauce

1 tsp smoked paprika

¼ tsp pure maple syrup

1 tsp liquid smoke

⅛ tsp ground sea salt

⅛ tsp ground black pepper

½ tsp extra-virgin olive oil

1 fresh pineapple

Lime wedges

Put the tofu on a plate lined with paper towels. Put a few layers of paper towels on top of the tofu and place something heavy on top to press the excess liquid out of the tofu for approximately 20 minutes. Slice the tofu into 1-inch (25-mm) cubes.

Whisk the soy sauce, paprika, maple syrup, liquid smoke, salt and pepper together until the paprika dissolves. Put the tofu cubes on a rimmed baking sheet and pour the marinade over them. Turn the cubes so all sides are soaked in the mixture and refrigerate for at least an hour. The longer you marinate them, the more intense the bacon flavor will be. We prefer to marinate the tofu overnight.

Preheat the oven to 400°F (204°C) and lightly grease a baking sheet with the olive oil.

Cut the stem and the bottom off of the pineapple, then cut the peel off. Remove the core and cut the fruit into 1 inch (25-mm) cubes. Alternate putting the tofu and pineapple squares on skewers and place the skewers on the oiled baking sheet. Roast for approximately 15 to 20 minutes, or until the pineapple begins to caramelize and the tofu is golden brown. Flip the skewers halfway through roasting. For added flavor, squeeze the juice from a lime wedge on top.

Serve as an appetizer or over a bed of Cheesy Grits (page 130) or jasmine rice as a meal.

Steak on a Stick

★ ★ ★ ⚑ ✕ ⚑ ★ ★ ★

Tofu steaks marinated in homemade steak sauce are the ultimate party food. This recipe is so easy to make and so tasty. All you need to do is whip up the sauce, marinate the tofu and grill them to a chewy perfection. The sauce gives the tofu a slightly tangy, savory umami flavor, and grilling gives them a slight char that adds even more BBQ flavor. You can also bake the steaks in a 375°F (191°C) oven for 15 minutes if you'd like. Make sure you save some of the sauce for dipping! Serve these next to our Southern-Style Creamy Potato Salad (page 117) and our Smoky Skillet BBQ Baked Beans (page 138).

SERVES 4

12 oz (340 g) extra-firm tofu

⅓ cup (80 ml) low-sodium soy sauce

¼ cup (60 ml) apple cider vinegar

3 tbsp (45 ml) ketchup

1 tbsp (15 ml) vegan Worcestershire sauce

1 tbsp (15 ml) prepared yellow mustard

1 tsp smoked paprika

2 tsp (9 g) brown sugar

½ tsp onion powder

Salt and pepper to taste

1 tbsp (15 ml) extra-virgin olive oil

Flatleaf parsley, finely diced, for topping

Put the tofu on a plate lined with paper towels. Put a few layers of paper towels on top of the tofu and place something heavy on top to press the excess liquid out of the tofu for approximately 20 minutes.

Whisk the soy sauce, vinegar, ketchup, Worcestershire sauce, mustard, paprika, sugar and onion powder together until well combined.

Slice the tofu into ½-inch (1.3-cm)-thick pieces and put them in a shallow baking dish with all but 2 tablespoons (30 ml) of the marinade. Turn the tofu to coat all sides and refrigerate for at least 1 hour. Reserve the extra marinade for dipping.

Slide a skewer lengthwise into each steak and add salt and pepper to taste. Heat a grill pan or skillet on medium heat and brush with the olive oil. Cook for 4 to 5 minutes per side, or until they're golden brown. Dip in the reserved sauce. Sprinkle with the parsley for added flavor.

Spicy BBQ Bean Balls

★ ★ ★ 🍴 ★ ★ ★

We've never met a bean ball that we didn't like—but these, they're our favorite. Without the right ratio of fat, black bean balls can be really dry if they're cooked too long. Not these. The addition of the olive oil and cashew butter prevents them from drying out and gives them extra sizzle and crispness on the exterior. These are a great party, tailgate or cozy-night-in appetizer. Dipping them in BBQ sauce is a must! If you want to make a meal out of these, pair them with our Smoky Grilled Broccoli (page 125) and our Baby Potato Packets with Lemon and Dill (page 110).

MAKES APPROXIMATELY 14 BALLS

1 tsp extra-virgin olive oil, plus more for oiling the grill pan

1 cup (75 g) chopped mushrooms

1 (15-oz [425-g]) can black beans

1 tbsp (15 g) cashew butter

¼ cup (4 g) cilantro leaves

1 tbsp (8 g) chili powder

½ tsp onion powder

½ tsp garlic powder

1 tsp smoked paprika

1 tbsp (15 ml) vegan Worcestershire sauce (we use Annie's brand)

1 tsp ground sea salt

½ tsp black pepper

¼ cup (38 g) cornmeal

¼ cup (28 g) brown rice flour

2 tbsp (30 ml) aquafaba

1 cup (240 ml) Big Mama's Homemade BBQ Sauce (see page 161) or store bought, divided

Heat the olive oil in a medium skillet on medium heat. When the oil is hot (test with a piece of the mushroom, it should sizzle), add the mushrooms and cook, stirring frequently, for approximately 5 to 7 minutes, or until they've lost their water and are golden brown. Transfer to a food processor.

Drain the beans (reserve the aquafaba) and rinse well. Process the beans, mushrooms, cashew butter, cilantro, chili powder, onion powder, garlic powder, paprika, Worcestershire sauce, salt and pepper in a food processor until the beans are mostly creamy. Transfer to a large mixing bowl.

Add the cornmeal, brown rice flour and aquafaba to the bean mixture and stir until well combined. Scoop 1 heaping tablespoon (15 g) of the mixture, squeeze together in your hands and roll into a solid ball. Continue with the rest of the mixture.

Heat a grill pan or skillet on medium-high heat and brush it with oil. When the pan is hot, add the bean balls and cook for approximately 1 minute per side, or until the surface of the balls is browned and crispy, approximately 6 to 7 minutes each side. Roll the balls in ½ cup (120 ml) of the BBQ sauce until coated. Arrange them on a pretty platter, insert a serving pick in each one, and serve with the remaining BBQ sauce for dipping.

Savory Veggie Skewers

These are so much better than your average veggie skewers. The rainbow of colors creates such a fantastic presentation and the fresh herbs, garlic and tangy balsamic vinegar take the marinade to another level. These are delicious with our Cheesy Grits (page 130).

SERVES 4

2 medium zucchini

1 medium red onion

2 medium orange bell peppers

1 small eggplant

1 medium summer squash

1 cup (240 ml) aged balsamic vinegar

1 tbsp (15 ml) liquid smoke

¼ cup (60 ml) soy sauce

3 tbsp (45 ml) extra-virgin olive oil

2 cloves garlic, minced

1 tbsp (15 g) chopped fresh rosemary leaves

1 tbsp (15 g) chopped fresh Italian oregano leaves

1 tsp brown sugar

1 tsp salt

1 tsp black pepper

Chop the zucchini, red onion, bell peppers, eggplant and summer squash into ½-inch (13-mm) cubes and place in an airtight container. Combine the balsamic vinegar, liquid smoke, soy sauce, olive oil, garlic, rosemary, oregano, brown sugar, salt and black pepper, and pour over the veggies. Place the veggies in the fridge for 2 hours, tossing them every half hour.

Skewer the veggies while heating up a grill pan or skillet to medium-high heat. Cook the veggies for approximately 5 to 8 minutes per side, or until they begin to brown and have dark grill marks.

You can also roast these in a 375°F (191°C) oven for approximately 30 minutes, or until the vegetables are caramelized.

Smoky Peach and Bourbon Chik'n Skewers

This is the perfect easy dinner for a summer night. The sweet peaches pair perfectly with the bourbon, black pepper and brown sugar glaze on the seitan. Enjoy it with a side of our Smoky Grilled Broccoli (page 125).

SERVES 4

1 (8-oz [226-g]) package seitan

¼ cup (50 g) brown sugar

1 tsp liquid smoke

2 tbsp (30 ml) bourbon

1 tsp salt

1 tsp black pepper

2 peaches

Cut the seitan into 1-inch (25 mm) cubes and put it into an airtight container. In a bowl, mix the brown sugar, liquid smoke, bourbon, salt and black pepper. Add the mixture to the container and shake until the seitan is covered. Place it in the fridge for an hour to marinate.

While the seitan is marinating, cut the peaches into ½-inch (13-mm) cubes. Skewer the seitan and the peaches, alternating the pieces.

Heat a grill pan or skillet to medium-high heat. Cook the skewers for 6 minutes per side. Or, roast in a 375°F (191°C) oven for approximately 30 minutes, or until the peaches are caramelized.

CHAPTER 4

★ Stuffed, Foiled and ★ Smothered: Delectable Entrees for a Cozy Dinner

How can you not be seduced by the food descriptions *stuffed* and *smothered*. You know that those two foodie terms can only mean good things. They mean lots of flavor, tons of decadence and the ultimate satisfying meal.

In this chapter, you'll find BBQ Buffalo Chick'n Pizza (page 102) smothered in our homemade BBQ sauce, and Mom's BBQ Cauliflower Stuffed Peppers (page 106), one of our testers' favorites. If it can be stuffed, foiled or smothered, it's in this chapter, so dig in!

Grilled Potato Steaks with Bacon and Vegan Sour Cream

This recipe is for our baked potato lovers. We've taken the classic baked potato and turned it into a grilling specialty that you can eat as a meal or serve as an appetizer. Grilling the potato steaks on a grill pan adds a nice smoky flavor that you can't get from baking. We left the skins on for added texture and vitamins, and topped them with the classic sour cream and chives. We also added a special little treat, vegan bacon bits. These go great with our BBQ Short Ribz (page 29). This is a simple and easy recipe that you can make on a busy weeknight or for a casual weekend meal.

SERVES 4 TO 6

2 large baking potatoes

1 tbsp (15 g) sea salt

2 tbsp (30 ml) vegan Worcestershire sauce

1 tbsp (15 ml) mesquite liquid smoke

2 tsp (10 ml) extra-virgin olive oil

Ground salt and pepper to taste

TOPPINGS

Vegan sour cream, or our Vegan Aioli (page 170)

Vegan bacon bits

Chopped chives

Slice the potatoes into ½-inch (13-mm)-thick steaks and put in a large pot of water with the salt. Bring to a boil. Once the water is boiling, cook for approximately 7 to 10 minutes or until you can pierce the potatoes to the center with a fork. They should be firm, yet tender, but not soft. Remove from the water and let cool.

In a measuring cup, whisk the Worcestershire sauce and liquid smoke together.

Heat a grill pan or skillet on medium-high heat and brush the oil over the surface. Brush both sides of the potato steaks with the Worcestershire sauce mixture and sprinkle with salt and pepper to taste. Cook the potatoes for approximately 5 to 7 minutes per side, or until they're golden brown with distinct grill marks.

Top with a dollop of vegan sour cream or aioli, and sprinkle with the vegan bacon bits and chives.

NOTE: McCormick Bacon Bits are vegan.

★ ★ ★

Teriyaki BBQ Meatloaf

★ ★ ★ ⚞ ✗ ⚟ ★ ★ ★

Take a little trip across the Pacific, but make sure to bring the South with you. This Teriyaki BBQ Meatloaf takes an Asian twist on a Southern classic. It keeps all of the savory notes of traditional loaves, and adds some new and unexplored meatloaf flavors. Add a side of our Collard Greens (page 137) and Spicy Grilled Corn on the Cob (page 118).

MAKES APPROXIMATELY 1 (9-INCH [23-CM]) LOAF

1 tbsp (15 ml) olive oil

1 medium white onion, diced

1 (15-oz [425-g]) can chickpeas

1 (15-oz [425-g]) can pinto beans

1 (15-oz [425-g]) can great northern beans

1 cup (125 g) panko breadcrumbs

¾ cup (90 g) cornmeal

2 cloves garlic, minced

½ cup (120 ml) aquafaba from chickpeas

1 tbsp (15 g) black sesame seeds

½ cup (120 ml) teriyaki sauce

½ cup (120 ml) soy sauce

¼ cup (50 g) brown sugar

1 tsp liquid smoke

¾ tsp white pepper

Juice of ½ lime

1 tbsp extra-virgin olive oil

Preheat the oven to 350°F (176°C).

In a sauté pan, heat the oil on medium-high heat. Toss in the onion and sauté until golden brown. Remove from the pan and set aside.

Drain (reserve the aquafaba) and rinse the chickpeas, pinto beans and great northern beans. Process half the beans in a food processor until creamy. Add the second half and pulse about five times or until slightly chunky. Remove the beans from the food processor and place into a large bowl. Fold in the panko, cornmeal, garlic, aquafaba and onions.

In a small bowl, mix the sesame seeds, teriyaki sauce, soy sauce, sugar, liquid smoke, pepper and lime juice until a uniform sauce forms. Fold all except ¼ cup (60 ml) of the sauce into the bean mixture until fully combined.

Prepare a loaf pan by brushing the olive oil on all sides. Press the mixture into the loaf pan and bake it for 55 to 65 minutes. Remove from the oven and allow the loaf to set for 15 minutes before serving. Brush with the remaining BBQ sauce.

Smoky Mac 'n' Cheese with Coconut Bacon

★ ★ ★ ═ ✕ ═ ★ ★ ★

When we think of Southern comfort food, we think of mac 'n' cheese. This decadent and soul-warming dish is a favorite in the South and the Midwest, especially at backyard BBQs. This is why we had to remake the standard mac 'n' cheese into a vegan version. The cashew cheese makes it just as creamy and comforting as dairy cheese, only a whole lot healthier. And don't skip the coconut bacon, because it adds that "sumpin sumpin" that only bacon flavor can.

SERVES 4

1 cup (60 g) unsweetened coconut flakes

2 tbsp (30 ml) liquid smoke

3 cups (720 ml) water

½ cauliflower head, chopped into small florets

½ cup (56 g) raw cashews soaked overnight in ½ cup (120 ml) water

1 cup (240 ml) unsweetened almond milk

Juice of ½ lemon

1 cup (160 g) nutritional yeast

1 clove garlic

½ tsp garlic powder

½ tsp smoked paprika

½ tsp salt

½ tsp black pepper

1 lb (453 g) cavatappi noodles

1 tbsp (15 ml) extra-virgin olive oil

½ cup (45 g) breadcrumbs

2 green onions, chopped

Preheat the oven to 350°F (176°C) and line a rimmed baking sheet with parchment paper.

Mix the coconut flakes with liquid smoke and spread them evenly on a lined baking sheet. Bake the coconut for approximately 7 minutes, or until golden brown. Remove them from the oven and then set aside.

Boil the water in a small pot. Once boiling, add the cauliflower and boil for 15 minutes. Drain the cooked cauliflower and place in a high-speed blender or food processor. Drain and rinse the cashews, and add to the food processor with the almond milk and lemon juice, then blend on high until smooth and creamy. Add the nutritional yeast, garlic, garlic powder, paprika, salt and pepper to the cashew cream and blend until well incorporated into the cashew–cauliflower mixture. Set aside.

Cook the pasta according to the package instructions. Mix in the cashew–cauliflower mixture and pour into a baking dish. Combine the olive oil and breadcrumbs together and sprinkle on top of the noodles.

Set the oven to broil, place the mac 'n' cheese on the top rack of the oven and broil for 5 to 10 minutes, or until the breadcrumbs turn golden brown. Serve by topping the mac 'n' cheese with the coconut bacon and green onions.

BBQ Buffalo Chick'n Pizza

* * * ≡ ✕ ≡ * * *

Who doesn't love a delicious BBQ pizza? This pizza combines our favorite aspects of BBQ cuisine including BBQ seitan (chik'n, or fake chicken), ranch dressing, bell peppers, shallots, buffalo sauce and crisp chives. Serve them up as a filling dinner for your family, or offer them as slices or mini pizzas to guests for a unique appetizer. Add our Grilled Wedge Salad with Vegan Ranch Dressing (page 133) to this for a complete meal.

MAKES APPROXIMATELY 2 (10-INCH [25-CM]) PIZZAS

1 cup (240 ml) warm water

1 (7 g) packet active dry yeast

1 tbsp (12 g) sugar

2 cups (240 g) all-purpose flour, divided

1 tbsp (15 g) Bragg's Sprinkle Seasoning

2 tsp (10 g) salt

3 tsp (15 ml) extra-virgin olive oil, divided

1 (8-oz [226-g]) package prepared seitan

¼ cup (60 ml) Have-It-Your-Way Chipotle BBQ Sauce (page 162) or store bought

½ cup (120 ml) Vegan Buttermilk Ranch Dressing (page 166) or store bought

1 cup (113 g) vegan mozzarella (we like Miyokos brand)

¾ cup (130 g) diced red bell pepper

2 shallots, thinly sliced

2 tbsp (30 ml) Smoky, Buttery Buffalo Sauce (page 174)

4 tbsp (12 g) chopped chives

Combine the water, yeast and sugar in a small bowl and let it sit for 5 minutes. If it doesn't bubble, the yeast isn't active, and you'll need to start over with new yeast. In a stand mixer with the dough hook attachment, combine the yeast mixture with 1½ cups (190 g) of flour, the Sprinkle Seasoning and salt until well combined with a sticky dough texture. Form the dough into a ball, coat with 1 teaspoon of olive oil, place in a bowl in a warm place and cover with a towel. Allow the dough to rise for 45 minutes.

While the dough is rising, put the seitan in a food processor and pulse until small crumbles form. Remove from the food processor and mix with the BBQ sauce. Set aside.

After the dough is done rising, preheat the oven to 425°F (218°C).

On a clean counter, dust ¼ cup (32 g) of flour and place half of the dough on the floured surface. Punch it down and knead it until the dough feels solid, approximately 2 minutes. Add ¼ cup (32 g) of flour to the surface and repeat with the second piece of dough. Roll both pieces of dough out on parchment lined pans into whatever shape you would like with ½ inch (1.3 cm) thickness.

Spread the ranch dressing on top of the crusts and then add slices of mozzarella, the BBQ seitan, bell peppers and shallots. Bake for 18 minutes. Drizzle the buffalo sauce and sprinkle the chives all over the pizza.

Southern Boil Grill Packets

These adorable and easy grill packets are the perfect dish for both a backyard BBQ or a casual weeknight dinner. All you have to do is toss in the ingredients and let your oven do the hard work. We love these with any of our burgers, or with our Spicy BBQ Bean Balls (page 89).

SERVES 4

12 fingerling potatoes

2 ears corn

1 (8-oz [227-g]) package prepared seitan

1 tsp Old Bay Seasoning

½ tsp onion powder

1 tsp liquid smoke

2 cloves garlic, minced

Preheat the oven to 400°F (204°C). Cut 8 pieces of 6 × 6-inch (15 × 15-cm) aluminum foil.

Quarter the potatoes and cut each ear of corn in half. Divide the potatoes, corn and seitan among 4 pieces of foil. Evenly sprinkle the vegetables with the Old Bay, onion powder, liquid smoke and garlic.

Place the remaining pieces of foil over the food and form into packets. Shake the packets until the ingredients are well incorporated. Slice a steam vent on the top of each packet and place into the oven. Bake for 45 minutes. Allow the packets to cool slightly before serving.

Mom's BBQ Cauliflower Stuffed Peppers

★ ★ ★ ⫤ ✕ ⫣ ★ ★ ★

My mom Mary, Alex's grandma, made the best stuffed peppers ever! We've never met one that even came close in flavor. We've taken the essence of her recipe and turned it into a BBQ lover's dream. We've also made them healthier and lighter because they're completely veggie. Serve them with our Southern-Style Skillet Cornbread (page 129) for a completely perfect down-home meal.

SERVES 4

4 bell peppers, any color

Olive oil, for brushing the peppers

1 cauliflower head

2 small ears corn, approximately 1½ cups (220 g) kernels

1 (15-oz [425-g]) can black beans, drained and rinsed

1 red onion, diced

1 jalapeño pepper, seeded and diced

2 tbsp (30 g) tomato paste

1 tbsp (15 ml) vegan Worcestershire sauce (we use Annie's brand)

½ cup (8 g) cilantro, stems removed, plus more for garnish

2 cloves garlic, minced

1 large tomato, cored and finely diced

1 tsp ground sea salt (add more if you like)

1 tbsp (8 g) chili powder

1 tsp smoked paprika

Black pepper to taste

1 cup (240 ml) Have-It-Your-Way Chipotle BBQ Sauce (page 162) or store bought

Preheat oven to 400°F (204°C) and line a rimmed baking sheet with parchment paper.

Cut the tops off of the peppers (reserve for later) and remove the core and seeds. Brush the olive oil over the surface of the peppers and the tops, place the peppers (open side down) and tops on the baking sheet and roast for approximately 20 minutes or until they begin to brown and blister. Remove from the oven and reduce the heat to 375°F (191°C).

Remove the core of the cauliflower and cut into small florets. Put them in a food processor (you may need to do this in batches) and pulse until they resemble rice. Scrape the cauliflower rice into a large skillet.

Cut the corn kernels off of the cobs and add to the skillet. Put the beans in the skillet, add the onion and jalapeño and stir to combine. Turn the heat on to medium and dry roast the vegetables for 5 minutes, stirring frequently. Add the tomato paste, Worcestershire sauce, cilantro, garlic, tomato, salt, chili powder, paprika and pepper, stir well and cook for 5 minutes.

Put the peppers in a 2-quart (2-L) round dish and stuff with the filling. Tightly cover with foil and bake for 20 minutes. Leave the tops aside and place them on top of the stuffed peppers before serving. There will be extra filling left over, so plate the stuffed peppers on a bed of the filling, spoon BBQ sauce on top and garnish with a sprig of fresh cilantro.

Loaded BBQ Potatoes

Potatoes have to be one of the most versatile vegetables on the planet. They make delicious soup, crunchy chips, savory fries and fluffy mashed potatoes. However, they're probably the most famous for their role as the baked potato. Here we've taken this classic recipe and transformed it into a vegan BBQ delight. The filling has a wonderful meaty texture, thanks to the jackfruit and the chipotle. Just one large potato can make a meal.

SERVES 4

4 large russet potatoes

2 tsp (10 ml) extra-virgin olive oil

¼ cup (19 g) unsweetened coconut flakes

2 tbsp (30 ml) liquid smoke

1 tsp salt

1 (14-oz [400-g]) can young jackfruit

½ cup (120 ml) Have-It-Your-Way Chipotle BBQ Sauce (page 162) or store bought

½ cup (56 g) vegan cheddar shreds, plus more for topping

2 green onions, chopped

1 large tomato, diced

½ cup (120 ml) Vegan Buttermilk Ranch Dressing (page 166) or store bought

Preheat the oven to 350°F (176°C).

Wash the potatoes and pierce each one with a knife approximately ten times. Coat the potatoes in the olive oil, place on a baking sheet, and bake in the oven for 50 to 70 minutes, or until easily pierced with a fork.

In a medium bowl, mix the coconut, liquid smoke and salt until combined and spread evenly on a baking sheet lined with parchment paper. Bake at 350°F (176°C) for 7 minutes, or until golden brown. Remove from the oven and let stand.

Rinse the jackfruit and pull the pieces with forks until the texture resembles pulled meat. Combine the jackfruit with the BBQ sauce and set aside.

Remove the potatoes from the oven, cut in half and squeeze open. Stuff the jackfruit into each potato and sprinkle the cheese on top. Bake the potatoes for another 20 minutes.

To serve, top the potatoes with green onions, tomatoes, coconut bacon, more cheddar and a dollop of our Vegan Buttermilk Ranch Dressing.

Baby Potato Packets with Lemon and Dill

★ ★ ★ ≡ ✕ ≡ ★ ★ ★

Oh, how we love to cook our food in little surprise packages. If you've ever had them, you know what we're talking about. It's like ripping open a birthday present, only there's steaming, delicious food inside. Wrapping up baby potatoes with a drizzle of olive oil, lemon slices, dill and shallots in parchment paper, then roasting them in the oven or grilling them on low heat is one of the easiest and most delicious ways to make potatoes. The parchment traps the steam and makes the potatoes so creamy. It also makes the lemon, dill and shallot flavors soak into the potatoes for an incredible, tasty dish. If you don't have parchment paper, you can wrap them in aluminum foil. These pair well with our Texas BBQ Brisket (page 26).

SERVES 4

3 lbs (1.4 kg) baby potatoes

1 tbsp (15 ml) extra-virgin olive oil

Sea salt and pepper to taste

1 large shallot, thinly sliced

1 lemon, cut into thin slices

2 to 4 sprigs fresh dill, minced

Preheat the oven to 400°F (204°C) and tear off four large squares of parchment paper.

Wash and scrub the potatoes, then cut them in half. Place in a large bowl and add the olive oil, salt and pepper, then toss to coat the potatoes. Divide the potatoes by 4 and place them in the center of the parchment squares. Sprinkle the shallot slices on top, then add the lemon slices and minced dill (we love dill so we add 4 sprigs, if you don't like a strong dill flavor add 2 or 3 sprigs).

Fold the parchment paper in half over the potatoes. Fold the left corner over, fold the side next to the corner over and then fold the next side over. Keep folding in that order until you get to the corner on the other side and tuck that over. Flip the packet over so it stays shut and place them in a roasting pan or on lined baking sheet to save your oven from any spillage. Roast for 50 minutes.

Southern Sticky Grilled Tofu

A Southern BBQ staple is sticky chicken. The star of the show is the sweet, tangy, sticky sauce. Without that, you just have a boring protein. The sauce in this recipe has a bright and sour burst of lime juice that adds the perfect acidity to the warmth of the other ingredients. We replaced the chicken with tofu, because it absorbs the flavor of the sauce so well, and we love its chewy texture. Serve this with our Carolina Coleslaw (page 121) and our Southern-Style Skillet Cornbread with Maple Butter (page 129).

SERVES 4

10 oz (284 g) extra-firm tofu, drained

¼ cup (56 g) brown sugar

1 clove garlic, minced

¼ cup (60 ml) water

2 tbsp (31 g) tomato paste

Juice of ½ lime

1 tbsp (15 ml) Worcestershire sauce

1 tbsp (15 ml) liquid smoke

1 tsp extra-virgin olive oil

Press the excess water out of the tofu by putting the tofu on a plate lined with paper towels, putting more towels on top of the tofu and placing something heavy, like an iron skillet, on top of the tofu. Let it sit for 20 minutes.

Slice the tofu through the center so you have two large, thin pieces, then slice each half into 1-inch (25-mm) rectangles. Slice the rectangles into cubes.

In a blender, blend the brown sugar, garlic, water, tomato paste, lime juice, Worcestershire sauce and liquid smoke on high until you have a thick and sticky sauce.

Pour half of the sauce onto a large rimmed baking sheet and place the tofu on top of the sauce. Pour the remaining sauce over the tofu and turn to coat all sides. Marinate the tofu for a minimum of 1 hour in the refrigerator.

Set the grill pan or skillet to medium-high heat and brush with the oil. When the pan is hot, add the tofu and cook for approximately 2 minutes per side, or until grill marks appear and the tofu is nicely seared and is heated through to the center.

CHAPTER 5

Sides and Salads That
★ Go with a Barbecue ★

Vegans, vegetarians and anyone with food allergies know that sides are where it's at. For those of us without veggie-centric families, you can find us at family gatherings and parties loading up on all the sides. You may as well call us side-a-vores. Because of this, we've learned that the sides should be just as important and captivating as the main dish, which is exactly what we've done here.

You'll find this chapter is filled with salads, like our Southern-Style Creamy Potato Salad (page 117) and Carolina Coleslaw (page 121). It also has old favorites, such as Cheesy Grits (page 130) and Southern-Style Skillet Cornbread with Maple Butter (page 129). Of course, there are some simple veggie dishes that you can whip up in no time, like our Smoky Grilled Broccoli (page 125) and Spicy Sweet Potato Wedges (page 134). So, go ahead side-a-vore! Load up on all these heavenly sides. You won't be left hungry.

Southern-Style Creamy Potato Salad

* * * = ✗ = * * *

If you want a taste of summer, of all things 4th of July and picnics at the beach, make our creamy potato salad. This big bowl of crazy deliciousness needs to be seated right next to every one of our vegan ribz, brisket and pulled BBQ recipes. It goes with everything, and will be the side dish hit of your next barbecue. What makes this potato salad Southern is the dill pickle juice and the chopped dill pickles. They add so much flavor and extra crunch to the creamy potatoes. This goes well with our Wisconsin-Style Grilled Bratwurst (page 66), any of our burgers and everything in between.

SERVES 6 TO 8

3 lbs (1.4 kg) Yukon Gold potatoes

2 tbsp (30 g) ground sea salt

1 cup (240 ml) vegan mayonnaise

2 tbsp (30 ml) Dijon mustard

2 tbsp (30 ml) dill pickle juice

1 tsp white wine vinegar

½ tsp sugar

¼ tsp garlic powder

¼ tsp onion powder

¾ cup (153 g) finely chopped dill pickle

2 ribs celery, finely diced

4 green onions, finely chopped

1 tsp paprika

Place the whole potatoes and the sea salt in a large pot of cold water (the water should cover the potatoes) and bring to a boil. Don't skip the salt. It is a vital component of the cooking process, as it allows the starch in the potatoes to fully cook, resulting in a creamier potato. Once the water is boiling, cook for approximately 12 to 15 minutes or until the potatoes are fork tender. You should be able to pierce them with a fork, but they shouldn't be fall-apart soft, so test them frequently. Drain the water and let the potatoes cool until you can safely handle them, approximately 10 to 15 minutes. Cut them into bite-size pieces and put them in a large serving bowl.

In a small bowl, whisk the mayonnaise, mustard, pickle juice, vinegar, sugar, garlic powder and onion powder until fully combined. Add to the potatoes, along with the chopped pickle, celery and green onions. Stir until the ingredients are fully combined and the potatoes are coated in the mayo mixture. Sprinkle with the paprika and chill in the refrigerator before serving.

Spicy Grilled Corn on the Cob with Cilantro Avocado Sauce

* * * ≡ ✕ ≡ * * *

This BBQ vegan take on Mexican street corn will bring you to your knees. No, I'm not exaggerating. This stuff is tangy, saucy, creamy, crunchy, salty and the perfect concoction for your BBQ. Don't be shy, slather on a liberal amount of the avo-cilantro sauce and Vegan Buttermilk Ranch Dressing (page 166). Pair this with our Spicy Grilled Crab Patties (page 45) or our Teriyaki BBQ Meatloaf (page 98).

SERVES 4

4 tbsp (56 g) vegan butter

2 tsp (10 ml) liquid smoke

1 tsp paprika

4 ears corn, shucked

1 avocado

1 cup (16 g) cilantro

Juice of 1 lime

2 tbsp (30 ml) white wine vinegar

¼ tsp salt

4 tbsp (40 g) nutritional yeast

¼ cup (60 ml) Vegan Buttermilk Ranch Dressing (page 166)

¼ cup (10 g) chopped Italian flat leaf parsley

3 tbsp (9 g) chopped fresh chives

Preheat the oven to 350°F (176°C).

Melt the vegan butter in the microwave for 30 seconds. Add the liquid smoke and paprika to the melted butter and stir until well combined. Brush a liberal amount on each ear of corn.

Place the corn on a baking sheet and bake for 20 minutes, or until it begins to brown.

While the corn is in the oven, place the avocado, cilantro, lime juice, vinegar and salt into a food processor and blend until completely smooth and creamy. Set aside.

Evenly spread the nutritional yeast on a plate.

Once the corn is done cooking, remove it from the oven and brush each ear of corn with the ranch dressing, roll in the nutritional yeast and finish by drizzling with avocado sauce and sprinkling with fresh parsley and chives.

Carolina Coleslaw

Coleslaw is another childhood favorite. You'll find this slaw in almost every Carolina restaurant worth its down home culinary salt. You can serve it as a side or pile it on your BBQ sandwich. Or, if you're like us, you'll just pile it on a plate and eat it as is.

Most slaws use regular green cabbage, but we decided to shake things up and use Napa cabbage, because we preferred the lighter texture. If you want to use green cabbage, go right ahead. It's all good. Serve this with any of our burgers, put it on top of our pulled BBQ sandwiches or serve with our Ribz (pages 18 and 29) and Texas BBQ Brisket (page 26). It goes with everything.

SERVES 6 TO 8

1 small green Napa cabbage, finely shredded

2 medium carrots, shredded

1 small Vidalia onion, thinly sliced

¼ cup (60 ml) white wine vinegar

1 tbsp (15 ml) Dijon mustard

1 tbsp (15 g) sugar

¼ tsp celery seed

2 tbsp (30 ml) extra-virgin olive oil

Salt and pepper to taste

Toss the cabbage, carrots and onion together in a large bowl to fully combine.

Whisk the vinegar, mustard, sugar, celery seed, olive oil, salt and pepper in a small bowl and pour on the vegetables. Toss to coat.

Chill for at least 1 hour for best results.

Mom's Creamy Cucumber Salad

My mom used to make this for every cookout and summer party our family ever hosted or attended. The smell of the fresh cucumbers filled our kitchen as she peeled and sliced them, and I couldn't wait to dig into that magical salad. My mom started adding sliced onions to her recipe after she married my dad, because that's how my paternal grandmother made hers. This salad is a combination of my mom's Southern roots and my dad's German heritage, and when I eat it, it feels like home.

The trick to a perfect creamy cucumber salad that doesn't get watery is patience. Once you've sliced the cucumbers, put them on a tray lined with paper towels and sprinkle them with a layer of salt, then let them sit for an hour. This will remove the excess water from the cucumbers to ensure a nice crisp crunch. This salad is awesome with our Old Bay Grilled Scallops (page 37).

SERVES 6 TO 8

3 large cucumbers, peeled and thinly sliced

2 tbsp + 1 tsp (35 g) ground sea salt, divided

¾ cup (180 ml) vegan mayonnaise, more if you like a really thick and creamy salad

1½ tsp (7 ml) extra-virgin olive oil

1 tbsp (15 ml) white wine vinegar

3 tbsp (45 ml) lemon juice

1 tsp ground black pepper

1 tbsp (13 g) sugar

1 small Vidalia onion, thinly sliced

½ cup (20 g) coarsely chopped dill, divided

Line a tray with paper towels and lay the cucumber slices over the towels. Evenly sprinkle 2 tablespoons (30 g) of sea salt over them and let sit for 1 hour. Pat the cucumbers dry with a paper towel (this will remove excess salt) and place in a large salad bowl.

In a medium mixing bowl, whisk together the mayonnaise, olive oil, vinegar, lemon juice, the remaining 1 teaspoon of salt, pepper and sugar until smooth and creamy.

Put the cucumbers, onion and half of the dill in a large bowl and pour the cream mixture on top. Gently fold until the cucumbers are completely coated. Sprinkle the remaining dill on top. Refrigerate for at least an hour before serving.

This is best if eaten the same day you make it.

Smoky Grilled Broccoli

This recipe will turn even the most adamant broccoli haters into broccoli lovers. The smoky, savory, salty flavor is so enticing that you won't be able to resist eating your veggies. The added bonus? It is by far one of the simplest and fastest recipes in this book. We love this side with our Spicy BBQ Bean Balls (page 89) and our Smoky Peach and Bourbon Chik'n Skewers (page 93).

SERVES 2 TO 4

1 large broccoli head, chopped into ½-inch (13-mm) florets

2 tbsp (30 ml) liquid smoke

3 tbsp (45 ml) teriyaki sauce

Juice of ¼ lime

1 tsp red pepper flakes (optional)

Preheat the oven to 400°F (204°C).

Combine the broccoli, liquid smoke, teriyaki sauce, lime juice and red pepper flakes in a large airtight container and shake the container until the broccoli is coated. Allow the broccoli to marinate for a minimum of 15 minutes.

Place the broccoli on a baking sheet and bake for 15 to 17 minutes, or until the broccoli begins to brown and is fork tender. Let it cool for 2 minutes before serving.

Roasted Lemon Dill Asparagus

When I was a kid, wild asparagus grew in a field near our house. I'd pick big bunches and take them home for my mom to steam because I loved this veggie so much. But it wasn't until I was an adult that I ventured into roasting asparagus. Thank goodness I stepped out of my box and changed my ways, because roasted is the way to go when it comes to cooking these delicious green spears. The high heat brings out the flavor and gives them a firmer bite. When you add the lemon and the dill to the mix, it's like eating a slice of spring. Happily, most supermarkets carry asparagus year-round, so we can eat it whenever the mood hits. We love to serve this with our Sizzling Mushroom Burgers (page 50).

SERVES 4

2 tbsp (30 ml) extra-virgin olive oil

Juice from 1 large lemon

1 bunch asparagus

Salt and pepper to taste

¼ cup (10 g) fresh dill, coarsely chopped

In a small bowl, whisk the olive oil and lemon juice together and set aside.

Cut the tough ends off of the asparagus stems, about ½ inch (1.3 cm) should be good. Put the asparagus in a roasting pan and drizzle with the oil and lemon juice mixture and salt and pepper to taste. Roll the asparagus to coat and let it marinate for 30 minutes.

Preheat the oven to 400°F (204°C).

Roast for 7 to 10 minutes (see note) and then roll the asparagus over and roast for another 7 to 10 minutes, or until the asparagus is pliable and begins to brown. Remove from the oven and sprinkle the dill over the asparagus while it's hot.

NOTE: Cook time will depend on how thick the asparagus is. Thinner stalks will take approximately 7 minutes on each side, thicker stalks may take 10 minutes per side.

★ ★ ★

Southern-Style Skillet Cornbread with Maple Butter

★ ★ ★ ═ ✕ ═ ★ ★ ★

True Southern cornbread shouldn't be sweet like a dessert bread. It should be savory, and you should be able to taste the corn in the cornmeal, not sugar. That's what you'll get when you make this bread. Instead of using oil, we melted vegan butter in the cast-iron skillet and then poured it into the batter. The result is a buttery, rich, melt-in-your-mouth cornbread. If you want to sweeten it up, make the maple butter and spread it on top. Cornbread goes so well with any of our ribz (pages 18 and 29), Texas BBQ Brisket (page 26) and BBQ Jerk Chik'n (page 42).

MAKES 1 (9-INCH [22-CM]) LOAF

1 tbsp (7 g) ground flax seed

3 tbsp (45 ml) water

1½ cups (190 g) all-purpose flour

1 cup (173 g) yellow cornmeal

2 tbsp (24 g) granulated sugar

2 tsp (8 g) aluminum-free baking powder

½ tsp ground sea salt

1 cup (240 ml) unsweetened almond milk

1 tbsp (15 ml) lemon juice

1 cup or 16 tbsp (116 g) vegan butter, divided

2 tbsp (30 ml) pure maple syrup

Preheat the oven to 400°F (204°C).

Whisk the ground flax seed and water together in a small bowl and let it rest while you prepare the dry ingredients.

Whisk the flour, cornmeal, sugar, baking powder and sea salt together in a large mixing bowl until they're completely combined.

Whisk the almond milk and lemon juice together in a measuring cup. It will lightly curdle.

Put ½ cup, or 8 tablespoons (58 g), of butter in a 10-inch (25-cm) cast iron skillet and melt it in the oven, approximately 3 minutes. Remove the pan from the oven, swirl the butter around to cover the surface and pour the rest of the butter into the dry mixture. Add the flax mixture and the almond milk mixture and stir until just combined. Scrape the batter into the skillet and spread evenly throughout the pan. Bake on a center rack for approximately 20 minutes or until the sides separate from the pan and a toothpick comes out clean when inserted in the center of the cornbread.

Whip 8 tablespoons (58 g) of vegan butter and the maple syrup until light and fluffy. Spread the maple butter on the cornbread.

Cheesy Grits

★ ★ ★ ⚎ ✗ ⚎ ★ ★ ★

Oh, how we love a hefty serving of cheesy grits. We love them for breakfast, lunch and dinner. It always breaks our hearts when we travel to the South and can't find a vegan version of our favorite side dish, so we had to create our own. Our recipe is made with unsweetened almond milk, vegan butter, a dash of chipotle chili powder and nutritional yeast to give it a nice cheddar flavor. It's just as creamy and dreamy as the grits we remember BV (before vegan). We always use old fashioned grits instead of instant—they just taste better. Grits are the perfect starch to serve with our Old Bay Grilled Scallops (page 37) or our Savory Veggie Skewers (page 90).

SERVES 4

3 cups (720 ml) unsweetened almond milk

1 cup (240 ml) water

1 tsp ground sea salt

1 cup (164 g) old fashioned grits

¼ tsp chipotle chili powder

1 tbsp (14 g) vegan butter

¼ cup (40 g) nutritional yeast

Chives, chopped (optional)

In a medium saucepan, bring the almond milk, water and salt to a boil and slowly whisk in the grits. Reduce the heat to low and simmer for approximately 15 minutes, or until the grits are thick and creamy. Stir often to avoid scorching. Remove from heat and stir in the chili powder, butter and nutritional yeast until the yeast is fully combined and the butter melts. Garnish with chopped chives if you like.

Grilled Wedge Salad with Vegan Ranch Dressing

✦ ✦ ✦ ═ ✗ ═ ✦ ✦ ✦

Wedge salads usually translate as high fat, low nutrient calorie bombs. However, we've transformed this typically unhealthy salad into a nutrient rich, satisfying, flavor-packed wedge. Bonus: To make this salad a meal, top it with some of our Southern Sticky Grilled Tofu (page 113)!

SERVES 4

¼ cup (19 g) coconut flakes

2 tbsp (30 ml) liquid smoke

⅛ tsp ground sea salt

1 romaine head, quartered with the stems still intact

1 tbsp (15 ml) olive oil

1 cup (240 ml) Vegan Buttermilk Ranch Dressing (page 166)

1 large tomato, diced

4 tbsp (12 g) chives

2 cups (480 ml) vegan ricotta cheese

Preheat the oven to 350°F (176°C) and line a rimmed baking sheet with parchment paper.

Mix the coconut flakes, liquid smoke and salt together. Bake the coconut mixture on the baking sheet for approximately 7 minutes, or until golden and toasty. Take it out of the oven and set aside.

Heat up a grill pan or skillet to medium-high heat. Brush the romaine quarters with the olive oil. Place the romaine on the grill with the cut side facing down. Grill for about 1 minute, just until grill marks appear, but make sure to remove the wedge before the leaves start to wilt. To finish off this decadent salad, pour some vegan ranch on top along with the coconut flakes, diced tomatoes, chives and vegan ricotta.

Spicy Sweet Potato Wedges

★ ★ ★ ═ ✕ ═ ★ ★ ★

If you love sweet potato fries, you're going to love these spicy sweet potato wedges. The sweetness in the potatoes tames the heat in our homemade jerk rub. You can pair them with all of the BBQ recipes in this book, or make them for an appetizer and dip them in one of our BBQ sauces. They're especially good with our Have-It-Your-Way Chipotle BBQ Sauce (page 162) or our Vegan Aioli (page 170).

SERVES 4

3 large sweet potatoes

3 tbsp (45 ml) extra-virgin olive oil

2 tbsp (30 g) Homemade Jerk Rub (page 178) or store bought

1 large lime

¼ cup (4 g) chopped cilantro leaves

Sea salt

Preheat the oven to 375°F (191°C).

Scrub the potatoes clean and slice them into thin wedges. The thinner you slice them, the faster they'll cook. Put the potato wedges in a large dish and toss with the oil and jerk rub until they're covered in the spices. Lay them flat on a large baking sheet and roast for approximately 25 minutes, or until they're fork tender. Flip midway through cooking. Squeeze a bit of fresh lime juice on top and garnish with chopped cilantro and sea salt.

Collard Greens with a Kick

Sunday afternoon supper always included some sort of greens at the table. These smoky and savory collard greens are definitely worthy of sitting alongside a big plate of ribz or vegan brisket, cornbread and creamy potato salad.

Collard greens are a tough green, so they need a long time to simmer, but aside from the time it takes to cook them tender, they're easy to make. To make chopping them go faster, stack several leaves, roll them up, and slice into ribbons, then cook them in the broth and enjoy the delicious aroma that will envelop your kitchen. Serve with our Teriyaki BBQ Meatloaf (page 98) or our Easy Peasy Black-Eyed Pea Burgers (page 61).

SERVES 4 TO 6

3 lbs (1.4 kg) fresh collard greens

1 tsp extra-virgin olive oil

1 large red onion, chopped

1¼ tsp (3 g) ground sea salt (divided)

3 cloves garlic, minced

32 oz (946 ml) vegetable broth

2 tbsp (30 ml) white wine vinegar

2 tsp (5 g) smoked paprika

Ground black pepper to taste

Vegan bacon bits (optional)

Wash and slice the leaves of the collard greens away from the thick part of the stem and coarsely chop the leaves.

Heat the oil in a 10-quart (10-L) Dutch oven or stock pot on medium heat and add the onions and ¼ teaspoon sea salt. Cook and stir frequently until the onions caramelize, approximately 5 minutes. Add the garlic and stir. Cook for 2 minutes. Add the collard greens and cook until the leaves begin to wilt, approximately 4 minutes. Add the broth, vinegar, paprika, 1 teaspoon of sea salt and pepper to taste and stir to combine. Bring to a boil, then reduce the heat to simmer and cook for approximately 1 hour, or until the greens are cooked to the tenderness of your liking.

Top with vegan bacon bits for extra flavor.

Smoky Skillet BBQ Baked Beans

* * * ≡ ✕ ≡ * * *

After one bite of these you'll never want canned baked beans again. They have just the right amount of sweetness and tenderness that you want in your baked beans. They also have a wonderful smoky flavor, like you'd find in beans with bacon, thanks to the small amount of liquid smoke that we added. We played around with the measurements of the brown sugar and molasses to make them healthier, and not as sweet as what you find in store-bought beans. We're confident that we got it just right.

You can make them in a Dutch oven or a casserole dish if you don't have an iron skillet, although iron heats so evenly that you might want to consider investing in one.

SERVES 4 TO 6

¼ cup (60 ml) maple syrup

¼ cup (56 g) brown sugar

2 tbsp (30 g) tomato paste

1 tbsp (15 ml) dark molasses

1 tbsp (15 ml) vegan Worcestershire sauce (we use Annie's brand)

1 tsp apple cider vinegar

1 tsp yellow mustard

½ tsp garlic powder

1 tsp liquid smoke

1 tsp extra-virgin olive oil

1 yellow onion, chopped

2 (15-oz [425-g]) cans navy beans (do not drain)

Preheat the oven to 325°F (163°C).

In a small bowl, whisk together the maple syrup, sugar, tomato paste, molasses, Worcestershire sauce, vinegar, mustard, garlic powder and liquid smoke until fully combined.

Heat the oil in a 10-inch (25-cm) cast iron skillet on medium-high heat. When the oil is hot, add the onions and stir to coat in the oil. Cook for approximately 5 to 7 minutes, or until they're slightly caramelized, stirring frequently to avoid scorching. Reduce the heat to low and add the beans with the liquid in the cans and the maple syrup mixture. Stir until well combined.

Put the cast iron skillet in the oven and bake uncovered on the middle rack for 30 to 45 minutes, or until the beans are thick and the sauce is sticky. The edges of the beans should be caramelized.

Smoky, Buttery Buffalo Cauliflower Bites

★ ★ ★ ═ ✗ ═ ★ ★ ★

May we just say that these little bite-sized delights can really get a party going! The tiny morsels of buffalo sauce–covered cauliflower are going to inspire you to cheer your favorite team on with ferocity! Perhaps a team with crimson and white? Plus, they're super easy to make, and we have never met a person who would turn them down. For a gluten-free recipe, substitute gluten-free beer and flour.

SERVES 4

1 large cauliflower head

1 cup (120 g) all-purpose flour

1 tsp garlic powder

1 tsp onion powder

½ tsp chili powder

1 tsp salt

2 tbsp (12 g) ground flaxseed

4 tbsp (60 ml) water

1 cup (240 ml) IPA beer

1 tbsp (15 g) lime zest

1 cup (240 ml) Smoky, Buttery Buffalo Sauce (page 174), divided

½ cup (120 ml) Vegan Buttermilk Ranch Dressing (optional, page 166)

Preheat the oven to 425°F (218°C).

Remove the core and break down the cauliflower into little nugget-size pieces, about the size of the tip of your thumb and set aside. Combine the flour, garlic powder, onion powder, chili powder and salt in a large bowl. In a separate bowl, mix the ground flaxseed, water, beer and lime zest together. Pour the liquid mixture into the dry ingredients and stir until well combined and a thick batter is formed.

Line a baking sheet with a non-stick surface (Silpat or parchment paper preferred). Dip the cauliflower bites in the batter one at a time and place on the baking sheet. Pop those little nuggets in the oven for 25 minutes.

Remove the cauliflower poppers from the oven and roll them in ½ cup (120 ml) of the buffalo sauce until completely covered. Serve with additional Smoky, Buttery Buffalo Sauce or Vegan Buttermilk Ranch Dressing for dipping.

CHAPTER 6

BBQ Dips to Bring to the Party

★ ★

How many times have you gone to a BBQ and had the center of attention, the best recipe there, the queen of all the dishes be the dip? Well, we know we have. Dips seem to be the dish that calls everyone to gather around and share in friendship, laughter and connection. Unfortunately, many dips leave the vegan crowd out due to cream, mayonnaise and other non-veggie-friendly ingredients.

Lucky for you, we've taken our favorite classic dips and given them vegan life! By replacing heavy cream with cashew cream, mayonnaise with our vegan aioli, and meat with ingredients such as jackfruit, we've taken dips above and beyond in an animal-friendly way. So, keep sharing and connecting with friends and family over this backyard staple with our creamy, enticing and oh-so-crazy-good vegan dips, such as our Buffalo Chik'n Dip (page 146), Jacked Up Crab Dip (page 145) and Grilled Artichoke Dip (page 150).

Jacked Up Crab Dip

* * * ⊜ ✕ ⊜ * * *

Crab dip is one of our favorite party dips. It's so creamy and mild in flavor, perfect for spreading on crackers or for dipping with your favorite veggies. Our vegan version is every bit as good as the conventional version. Shredded young jackfruit is surprisingly similar in texture to crab, and the flavors of the Dijon, Old Bay seasoning and the other spices are spot on. In case you're not familiar with Old Bay seasoning, let us acquaint you. Old Bay is a fragrant mix of spices, such as celery salt, mace, cloves, ginger, cardamom and more. It's what gives most crab cakes their flavor, and it's what brings this crab dip to life.

To get the texture and mouth feel of crab, we used shredded jackfruit, and the creaminess of mayonnaise comes from cashews. It's the ultimate party food. Bring this, and your appetite, to your next get together. You and your friends are going to love it! Serve with crackers, toasted sliced bread or corn chips.

SERVES 4 TO 6

2 cups (300 g) raw cashews, soaked in 2 cups (480 ml) water overnight

1 large clove garlic

¼ cup (60 ml) unsweetened cashew milk or other vegan milk

2 tbsp (30 ml) lemon juice

2 tbsp (30 ml) Dijon mustard

½ tsp Old Bay seasoning

½ tsp ground sea salt

¼ tsp ground paprika

⅛ tsp onion powder

1 (14-oz [400-g]) can young jackfruit packed in water or 1½ cups (400 g) fresh jackfruit

Drain and rinse the cashews and put into a high-powered blender or food processor. Add the garlic, cashew milk, lemon juice, mustard, Old Bay seasoning, salt, paprika and onion powder and blend for approximately 2 minutes (scrape the sides frequently), or until it's smooth and velvety. You shouldn't see or taste pieces of solid nuts.

Scrape the cashew mixture into a medium bowl.

Drain and rinse the jackfruit well. Shred the jackfruit with a fork or in a food processor and put in the bowl with the cashew mixture. Gently fold until fully combined. Serve with crackers, toast or sliced vegetables.

Buffalo Chick'n Dip

★ ★ ★   ☰   ✗   ☰   ★ ★ ★

If you ask most people in the Midwest, they'll tell you that they're buffalo chicken dip connoisseurs. In fact, I bet you most of them would be able to tell you the exact person who makes the best one and spend 20 minutes describing exactly what makes it the best. Maybe they will say their mom, their best friend or that guy who's always at the left side of the tailgate with that huge red grill . . . until now. We're not underselling this. Make this dip for your friends and you'll be their new favorite, all knowing, buffalo chick'n dip chef. Plus, no animals were harmed in the making of our buffalo chick'n dip. Serve with celery and/or carrot sticks, pita chips or corn chips.

SERVES 4 TO 6

1 cup (113 g) cashews soaked in 1 cup (240 ml) water overnight

Juice of ½ lemon

¼ cup (60 ml) water

¼ tsp paprika

½ tsp salt

⅓ cup (53 g) nutritional yeast

1 (14-oz [400-g]) can young jackfruit in water

½ cup (120 ml) Smoky, Buttery Buffalo Sauce (page 174)

⅓ cup (80 ml) Vegan Buttermilk Ranch Dressing (page 166)

¼ cup (13 g) chopped fresh chives

Preheat the oven to 425°F (218°C).

Drain and rinse the cashews and place them in a high-speed blender with the lemon juice, water, paprika, salt and nutritional yeast. Blend the cashews until smooth and creamy. Set aside.

Rinse the jackfruit well. Pull the pieces with two forks until the jackfruit resembles the texture of pulled chicken. In an oven-safe dish, mix the jackfruit with the buffalo sauce, ranch dressing and cashew cream. Bake the dip in the oven for 18 minutes. Let the dip cool slightly and sprinkle with the chives. Serve with crostini, chopped veggies or tortilla chips.

Smoky Blackened Corn Salsa

There is nothing like homemade corn salsa, especially when you make it with roasted fresh corn, jalapeños and onions. The smoky flavors of the vegetables, the sweetness of the corn and the tangy lime juice mingle together to create the most incredibly fresh salsa you'll ever eat.
Serve with corn chips or on burgers or tacos.

SERVES 4 TO 6

1 tbsp (15 ml) extra-virgin olive oil

3 ears corn, husks removed

2 jalapeño peppers

1 large red onion, sliced into ½-inch (13-mm) rounds

Juice of 1 lime

½ cup (8 g) cilantro, stems removed and chopped

½ tsp ground sea salt

⅛ tsp chipotle chili powder

Preheat the oven to 400°F (204°C) and line a rimmed baking sheet with parchment paper.

Brush the oil on the corn, jalapeño peppers and onion slices (both sides) and roast for approximately 20 to 25 minutes, or until the jalapeños and onion caramelize. Let cool.

Finely chop the roasted onion and put in a medium bowl. Remove the stems and seeds of the jalapeños and finely chop and put in the bowl with the onion. Put a corn cob in the bowl upright, and slice the kernels off from the top to the bottom, as close to the cob as you can get. Do the same with the remaining corn cobs. Add the lime juice, cilantro, salt and chili powder and stir to combine.

Serve chilled.

Grilled Artichoke Dip

★ ★ ★ ≡ ✕ ≡ ★ ★ ★

One of my fondest memories is visiting my grandmother, Linda's mother, and seeing a huge bowl of spinach and artichoke dip on the countertop. This was the staple of every holiday, family gathering and sporting event in our childhoods. Now, we've come up with a recipe that tastes just the same, if not way better, and doesn't include globs of mayonnaise, heavy cream and other unhealthy ingredients. Feel like you're treating yourself without disrupting your healthy lifestyle. Serve with toasted slices of bread, corn chips or veggie sticks.

SERVES 6 TO 8

1 (14-oz [40-g]) can quartered artichoke hearts, packed in water

1½ cups (169 g) raw cashews, soaked overnight in 1½ cups (360 ml) water

½ cup (120 ml) water

1 tbsp (15 ml) white wine vinegar

¼ cup (40 g) nutritional yeast

½ tsp garlic powder

1 tsp liquid smoke

¾ tsp white pepper

1 tsp ground sea salt

½ cup (15 g) chopped spinach

¼ cup (31 g) breadcrumbs

1 tbsp (15 ml) extra-virgin olive oil

Preheat oven to 425°F (218°C). Drain the artichoke hearts.

Heat a grill pan or skillet on medium-high heat. When the pan is hot, cook the artichokes for approximately 2 minutes per side, or until they're browned or have dark grill marks. Remove from the pan and let cool.

Drain and rinse the cashews and put them in a high-powered blender. Add the water, vinegar, nutritional yeast, garlic powder, liquid smoke, pepper and salt. Blend on a high speed until smooth and creamy.

Put the grilled artichokes in the blender and pulse until they're broken down into small pieces.

In a small casserole dish, combine the artichokes, spinach and cashew mixture and set aside while you prepare the breadcrumb mixture.

Mix the breadcrumbs and oil in a small bowl and evenly crumble over the dip. Bake for 12 to 15 minutes or until the breadcrumb topping is golden brown.

Charred Poblano Pepper Guacamole

★ ★ ★ ≡ ✗ ≡ ★ ★ ★

Our favorite guacamole recipe ever! Grilling the avocado adds depth to the flavor and even more creaminess to the fruit. The fire-roasted poblano pepper and the grilled onion add an intense smokiness and create one of the tastiest bowls of guacamole you'll ever eat. Slather it on burgers, put a dollop or two in your favorite taco or burrito, and of course, dip those chips into a bowl of this green goodness.

SERVES 6 TO 8

1 large poblano pepper

2 avocados

1 tsp avocado oil

1 small red onion, sliced into ½-inch (13-mm) rounds

¼ cup (4 g) fresh cilantro, coarsely chopped

Ground sea salt to taste

Juice of 1 small lime

2 tbsp (19 g) chopped red onion, for topping

Heat a grill pan or skillet on medium-high heat and roast the poblano pepper until its skin is blackened and blistered on all sides, approximately 10 minutes. Remove and let cool.

Slice the avocados in half and remove the pits. Brush a thin layer of avocado oil on the flesh of the avocados and grill flesh side down for approximately 3 minutes, or until they have distinct grill marks.

Brush the onion slices with a thin layer of oil and grill until they're caramelized, approximately 5 minutes. Flip and grill the other side for 5 minutes.

Scoop the flesh out of the avocado skins and put in a medium serving dish. Mash the avocado.

Scrape the blackened skin off of the poblano pepper and dispose of the skin, then remove the stem and the seeds. Finely dice and add to the avocado.

Finely chop the onion and add to the avocado and pepper mixture. Add the cilantro, salt and the lime juice. Stir to combine. Top with chopped raw red onion.

Tennessee Caviar

★ ★ ★ ═ ✕ ═ ★ ★ ★

You've probably heard of Texas Caviar, but it doesn't hold a candle to Tennessee Caviar. This fabulous and fresh dip is made with black-eyed peas. These pretty beans have a distinct earthy flavor that pairs perfectly with the sweet corn, spicy jalapeño and fresh tomato and cilantro. If ever a food could be called a party in your mouth, our Tennessee Caviar would be it. Serve with corn chips, pita chips or put on a burger.

SERVES 6 TO 8

2 ears sweet corn, husked, or 2 cups (293 g) frozen corn (thawed)

2 (15-oz [425-g]) cans black-eyed peas

1 small red onion, finely diced

1 jalapeño pepper, seeded and finely diced

1 large tomato, cored, seeded and finely diced

½ cup (8 g) fresh cilantro, coarsely chopped

¼ cup (60 ml) cup white wine vinegar

2 tsp (1 g) dried Italian seasoning

⅛ tsp ground sea salt

Pepper to taste

¼ cup (60 ml) extra-virgin olive oil

Preheat the oven to 375°F (191°C).

Roast the corn in a rimmed baking dish for approximately 20 to 25 minutes, or until some of the kernels begin to brown. Remove from the oven and let cool.

Drain and rinse the black-eyed peas well and put them in a large serving bowl. Put a corn cob in the bowl with the peas and cut the corn kernels off of the cob (do this over the bowl from the top down, as close to the cob as possible, to prevent kernels from flying off of the kitchen counter). Add the onion, jalapeño, tomato and cilantro to the bowl and gently toss until the ingredients are combined.

In a medium bowl, whisk the vinegar, Italian seasoning, salt and pepper until the salt is dissolved. Add the olive oil and whisk until the ingredients are completely combined. Pour over the corn mixture and toss to coat. Eat as a salad or as a dip with corn chips.

Ranch Dip with Grilled Crudités

This is a recipe to truly impress your friends. The grilled veggies with a myriad of colors, textures and flavors will entice your friends more so than your typical veggie platter. It's also incredibly easy to make.

SERVES 6 TO 8

8 baby multicolored carrots, with greens attached

15 small radishes, cut in half, with leaves attached

15 baby bell peppers

2 cups (170 g) snap peas

1 bunch asparagus

1 tbsp (15 ml) extra-virgin olive oil

1 cup (240 ml) Vegan Buttermilk Ranch Dressing (page 166)

Preheat a grill pan or skillet on medium-high heat. Brush the veggies with olive oil. Grill or sear the vegetables for approximately 5 minutes per side, or until they just start to turn soft. Be careful to not scorch the carrots' stems.

Arrange the grilled veggies around a bowl of the ranch dressing and serve.

CHAPTER 7

Keeping It Saucy: BBQ Sauces and Rubs

Let's face it, BBQ isn't BBQ without a good sauce, and boy do we love our sauces. Even though this is the last chapter in the book, these are the first recipes we developed. They're the glue that binds it all together.

You'll find Big Mama's Homemade BBQ Sauce (page 161), inspired by our maternal grandmother; Sweet Home Alabama White BBQ Sauce (page 165), created by our love of the Crimson Tide; Vegan Aioli (page 170), because you can't have a burger without it, and so much more.

Have you ever noticed how every sauce has its own unique personality? Seriously. From the light airiness of white wine sauce, to the deep and intense character of a chipotle sauce, each one has its own personality, and can take a good meal to divine. Whether you like mild, hot or somewhere in between, these sauces will give you the exact kick that your dishes are calling for.

Many sauces are known by the region, or state they were created in. Throughout this chapter, we're going to take a little tour of the U.S.A. from the creamy sauces of Alabama (page 165) to the zippy and spicy sauce of Virginia (page 161). The Carolinas have their own way of making BBQ sauce (page 162), so does New Orleans and more.

It's so easy to make your own sauce, there's really no need to buy it. One of the great things about making it from scratch is that you can control how much spice, sugar or salt goes into it. You can also make as little or as much as you'll need, which means no wasting.

Big Mama's Homemade BBQ Sauce

★ ★ ★ ≡ ✗ ≡ ★ ★ ★

Big Mama was my maternal grandmother's nickname. She loved to cook, lived in Virginia and made the best Southern food I've ever tasted. This sauce reminds me of her and brings back so many good memories of my childhood. Put it in or on anything that you'd put ketchup on, because it's so much better!

It's a little sweet, but not too sweet. It's a little tangy and a little savory. It plays well with others, so brush it or pour on your favorite burger, and always dip your fries in it.

MAKES 2 CUPS (480 ML)

½ tsp cornstarch

2 tbsp (30 ml) warm water

1 cup (240 ml) tomato sauce

2 tbsp (30 ml) tomato paste

3 cloves garlic or ¾ tsp garlic powder

¼ cup (60 ml) apple cider vinegar

2 tbsp (30 ml) dark molasses

1½ tsp (8 g) ground sea salt

¼ cup + 1 tbsp (46 g) coconut or dark brown sugar

½ tsp onion powder

1 tsp cumin

1 tsp ground paprika

½ tsp ground black pepper

1 tsp extra-virgin olive oil (optional)

In a small bowl, whisk the cornstarch and water together until smooth. You shouldn't see any lumps. Set aside.

Place the tomato sauce, tomato paste, garlic, vinegar, molasses, salt, sugar, onion powder, cumin, paprika, black pepper and olive oil into a blender or food processor and blend on high until smooth and frothy.

Pour the mixture into a small saucepan and bring to a boil. As soon as the sauce begins to boil, reduce the heat to a low simmer and cook for approximately 20 minutes. Stir frequently to prevent scorching. Slowly whisk the cornstarch into the sauce and keep whisking until the sauce thickens. Cook for 10 minutes, stirring frequently.

Store in an airtight container in the refrigerator for up to 2 weeks.

NOTE: If you have a Blendtec blender, use the Whole Foods/Soup setting.

★ ★ ★

Have-It-Your-Way Chipotle BBQ Sauce

★ ★ ★ ═ ✕ ═ ★ ★ ★

One of my favorite things about BBQ sauce is how the flavors vary from region to region. This heat-filled sauce reminds me of one that I used to eat when we went to the beach in South Carolina. It will slap your tongue if you let it. Add a lot of chipotle pepper and it might hurt a little. Add a little, and you'll be all right. In our family, we're not happy unless our BBQ sauce makes us break a sweat. We're weird like that, but we understand that most people are normal and don't want to cry when they eat, that's why we want you to have it your way. Make it as mild or as hot as you want, it's totally up to you.

MAKES 2 CUPS (480 ML)

½ tsp cornstarch

2 tbsp (30 ml) warm water

2 large red tomatoes or 2 cups (480 ml) canned tomato sauce

4 cloves garlic or 1 tsp garlic powder

⅓ cup (80 ml) apple cider vinegar

3 tbsp (45 ml) dark molasses

1½ tsp (8 g) ground sea salt

⅓ cup (48 g) coconut or dark brown sugar

1 tsp onion powder

1 tsp cumin

¼ to 1 tsp ground chipotle pepper (see note)

½ tsp ground black pepper (see note)

1 tsp extra-virgin olive oil (optional)

In a small bowl, whisk the cornstarch and water together until it's smooth and creamy.

Blanch the tomatoes in boiling water for approximately 2 minutes, or until the skin starts to separate from the meat. Remove from the water and let cool. Remove the skin and seeds and place in a high-powered blender or food processor. Add the garlic, vinegar, molasses, salt, sugar, onion powder, cumin, chipotle pepper, black pepper and olive oil to the blender. Blend on high until smooth and frothy.

Pour the mixture into a small saucepan and bring to a boil. As soon as the sauce begins to boil, reduce the heat to a low simmer and cook for approximately 20 minutes. Stir frequently to prevent scorching. Add the cornstarch mixture and whisk well until it thickens. Cook for another 5 to 8 minutes.

Store in an airtight container in the refrigerator for up to 2 weeks.

NOTE: If you're not a fan of spicy food, add the chipotle pepper and black pepper by the ¼ teaspoon until you get the desired heat that's right for you.

★ ★ ★

Sweet Home Alabama White BBQ Sauce

★ ★ ★ ═ ✗ ═ ★ ★ ★

What is a BBQ without some BBQ sauce? While most people think of sticky, sweet and dark when it comes to BBQ sauce, some of our friends down South have something different in mind. This Alabama inspired BBQ sauce is creamy, tangy and a little bit zippy. Most of all, it's the perfect addition to your next BBQ. Slather it on either of our seitan ribz (pages 18 and 29), drizzle on a baked potato (page 97) or dip some of our amazing cauliflower poppers (page 141) into this jaw-dropping sauce.

MAKES APPROXIMATELY 2 CUPS (480 ML)

2 cloves garlic

⅛ tsp extra-virgin olive oil

1½ cups (169 g) raw cashews, soaked overnight in 1½ cups (360 ml) water

Juice of 1 lemon

½ cup (120 ml) unsweetened plain almond milk

¼ cup (60 ml) white wine vinegar

2 tbsp (30 ml) horseradish mustard

½ tsp ground black pepper

¼ tsp paprika

½ tsp salt

Preheat the oven to 425°F (218°C). Wrap the unpeeled cloves of garlic and olive oil in aluminum foil and roast for 8 minutes. Remove from the oven and let cool. When the garlic is cool enough to handle, remove the skins.

Drain and rinse the cashews and place into a high-powered blender or food processor. Add the lemon juice, almond milk, vinegar, mustard, pepper, paprika and salt and blend on high until smooth and creamy.

Store in an airtight container in the refrigerator for up to 3 days. The cashews will thicken so you may have to add a bit of water and stir to thin the sauce.

Vegan Buttermilk Ranch Dressing

* * * ✖ * * *

Growing up in the Midwest, ranch dressing was in or on everything. However, the Meyer household was completely absent of this creamy concoction. Its unhealthy qualities were most likely the culprit. Now, thanks to our healthy and delicious vegan version, ranch dressing is back on the menu, and we love it!

MAKES APPROXIMATELY 1 CUP (240 ML)

1 cup (113 g) raw cashews, soaked overnight in 1 cup (240 ml) water

Juice of ½ lemon

1 tbsp (15 ml) white wine vinegar

½ cup plus 3 tbsp (165 ml) water

1 clove garlic

½ tsp ground sea salt

¼ cup (10 g) chopped Italian flat leaf parsley

3 tbsp (9 g) chopped fresh chives

Drain and rinse the cashews and put them in a high-speed blender or food processor. Add the lemon juice, vinegar, water, garlic and salt. Blend the mixture on high until the dressing is smooth and creamy, approximately 3 minutes.

Pour the cashew mixture into a medium bowl and stir in the parsley and chives until well combined.

Store in an airtight container in the refrigerator for up to 3 days. The cashews will thicken, so add a bit of water and stir until you get the desired consistency.

Horseradish Pesto

The horseradish in this pesto gives just the right kick. We love it on our milder flavored sandwiches, such as our Loaded Grilled Veggie Sandwich (page 81). It also makes a great dip or base for a spicy bruschetta. There's no wrong way to enjoy it.

MAKES APPROXIMATELY ¾ CUP (180 ML)

½ cup (86 g) almonds

1½ oz (42 g) fresh basil, stems removed

2 cloves garlic

1 tbsp (15 g) horseradish

1 tbsp (5 g) nutritional yeast

½ cup (120 ml) extra-virgin olive oil

¼ cup (60 ml) lemon juice

Ground sea salt and black pepper to taste

Toast the almonds in a hot pan until they turn a golden brown, approximately 5 minutes. Stir or shake frequently to ensure they brown evenly and don't scorch. Remove from the heat.

Put the almonds, basil, garlic, horseradish, nutritional yeast, olive oil, lemon juice, salt and pepper in a food processor and process until smooth and thick. It will be creamy, with some nuttiness to it.

Serve immediately, or store in an airtight container in the refrigerator for up to a week.

Vegan Aioli

* * * ≡ ✕ ≡ * * *

True French Mediterranean aioli is made with a mortar and pestle with garlic, salt, lemon juice and olive oil. We're convinced only culinary unicorns can turn those ingredients into aioli. After numerous attempts to make it with those four ingredients and a mortar and pestle, we ended up with sore arms and a mortar filled with oil and garlic paste. So, as stubborn women do, we decided that we'd add one more ingredient to the mix to ensure that you'd be able to make the creamiest, most delicious dressing to slather on whatever food you deem worthy. Say hello to our magical vegan aioli. Thank you, cashews.

MAKES 1 CUP (240 ML)

1 cup (112 g) cashews, soaked overnight in 1 cup (240 ml) water

4 cloves garlic, thinly sliced

¼ cup (60 ml) lemon juice

½ tsp ground sea salt, or more to taste

2 to 3 tbsp (30 to 45 ml) extra-virgin olive oil

Drain the cashews and rinse, then put in the blender with the garlic, lemon juice and salt. Blend on high speed until smooth and creamy, approximately 2 to 3 minutes. Scrape the sides if necessary. Add 2 tablespoons (30 ml) of the olive oil and blend until it's fully combined. If you want it to be thinner, add the additional 1 tablespoon (15 ml) of oil and blend well.

Store in an airtight container in the refrigerator for up to 3 days. The cashews will cause the aioli to thicken, so add a bit of water and stir until you get the desired consistency.

10-Minute Homemade Chimichurri

This gorgeous green sauce is so light, fresh and bright. The aroma of the fresh herbs and the zippy lemon takes us to our happy place. It's like eating a bite of sunshine. We put this on everything, especially spicy veggie burgers and salads.

MAKES ⅓ CUP (80 ML)

1½ cups (24 g) flat leaf parsley, stems removed

1 cup (16 g) cilantro leaves, stems removed

2 cloves garlic

½ tsp dried oregano

½ tsp red pepper flakes

½ tsp ground sea salt

2 tbsp (30 ml) olive oil

1 tbsp (15 ml) lemon juice

2 tbsp (30 ml) white balsamic vinegar

Ground black pepper to taste

Place the parsley, cilantro, garlic, oregano, red pepper flakes (see note), sea salt, olive oil, lemon juice, vinegar and black pepper in a blender or food processor and blend for 1 minute or until the parsley and cilantro are finely ground. If you like a thin sauce you can add a bit of water until you get the consistency you like.

Store in an airtight container for up to 4 days.

NOTE: If you don't like spicy food you can start with ⅛ teaspoon of red pepper flakes and add from there until you get the heat that's good for you, or just omit it.

★ ★ ★

Smoky, Buttery Buffalo Sauce

A staple of any tailgate, BBQ or grill out has to be buffalo sauce. Coat some "meat"-balls, wings or cauliflower poppers with this tangy, rich and spicy sauce.

MAKES APPROXIMATELY 1 CUP (240 ML)

½ cup (120 ml) melted vegan butter (we use Miyoko's or Earth Balance)

½ cup (120 ml) red hot sauce

2 tsp (10 ml) vegan Worcestershire sauce (we use Annie's)

2 tbsp (30 ml) white wine vinegar

½ tsp ground white pepper

¼ tsp liquid smoke

¼ tsp ground sea salt

In a medium bowl or a mason jar, combine the butter, hot sauce, Worcestershire sauce, vinegar, white pepper, liquid smoke and salt. Whisk until uniformly combined. Use immediately, or store in the fridge in an airtight container for up to a week. Melt in a small pan over low heat before serving.

Avocado Lime Sauce

Cool. Refreshing. Eat with a spoon. That's how we'd describe this pretty green sauce that you can smother almost anything with. Avocados and limes were meant to be together, and when you introduce creamy yogurt, cilantro and garlic to the mix, you're going to whip up one of the most delicious and light sauces you've ever had. Not only is this a great topping, it's also perfect as a creamy salad dressing.

MAKES 1 CUP (240 ML)

1 avocado

¼ cup (60 ml) plain unsweetened almond yogurt (we use Kite Hill brand)

3 tbsp (45 ml) lime juice

1 tbsp (1 g) cilantro leaves

1 clove garlic

½ tsp ground sea salt

Remove the pit from the avocado and scoop the flesh into a blender. Add the yogurt, lime juice, cilantro, garlic and salt, and blend on high until it's smooth and creamy, approximately 1 minute. Eat immediately.

Homemade Jerk Rub

★ ★ ★ ⚌ ✕ ⚍ ★ ★ ★

Jerk rub is used so frequently in our house that we make our own. It's a delightful blend of savory, earthy spices with a little bit of sugar for good measure. We love rubbing this on our tofu steaks, brisket or anything that requires a lot of flavor. It's fun to make your own jerk rubs because you can add a little extra something to make it uniquely yours. And, if you don't like a certain spice, you can always leave it out.

MAKES APPROXIMATELY ½ CUP (50 G)

¼ cup (32 g) chili powder

1 tbsp (2 g) ground cumin

2 tsp (4 g) ground nutmeg

2 tsp (4 g) ground cinnamon

1 tsp smoked paprika

1 tsp Italian seasoning

1 tsp ground sea salt

1 tsp brown sugar

½ tsp ground black pepper

¼ tsp cloves

¼ tsp cayenne pepper

Put all of the spices in a glass jar with a lid and shake the jar to mix the spices. If you don't have a jar you can use a fork to whisk them together in a bowl.

Store in an airtight container in a cool, dry place for up to 6 months.

★ Acknowledgments ★

Thank you to Will Kiester, Sarah Monroe and everyone else behind the scenes at Page Street Publishing for giving us the opportunity to make our dreams come true. You helped make the process of writing our first cookbook so much easier.

Thank you to Kelly Allison and her amazing team for making our cookbook visually stunning, and for making our recipes come to life. Your talent, generosity and spirit are amazing and infectious. Thank you to Carolyn Somlo for being Kelly's incredible agent and for being so kind to us throughout the journey. We've made new lifetime friends.

A big fat thank you and hug to the loyal and amazing readers of our blog. Without your support and love we wouldn't have been offered this opportunity. This, our friends, is for you!

Thank you to our friends who so willingly took the time to test our recipes and give us honest and meaningful feedback. Our recipes are better because of you.

Last but not least, thank you to Greg and Max, who cheered us on, stuffed their faces with whatever we put in front of them, and turned a blind eye to four months of chaos, tears and dirty dishes. We love you to the moon and beyond.

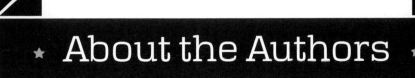

About the Authors

LINDA and **ALEX MEYER** are the mother-daughter duo behind the vegan blog, Veganosity. They started their vegan journey over three years ago after Alex chose to go vegan because of the health, environmental and ethical impacts of eating animal products. Linda was so inspired by Alex's new lifestyle that she soon chose to live a vegan lifestyle as well. A few months later, after reinventing their favorite recipes (vegan style), they created Veganosity so they could share their recipes with vegans and non-vegans.

Since they began their vegan journey, Alex has become a NASM-certified personal trainer, and received her Master's in Counseling Psychology with a concentration in Health Psychology. Linda is currently working on becoming certified in plant-based nutrition.

Veganosity's recipes have been featured in Bustle.com, *Shape*, thekitchn.com, FitnessMagazine.com, Bitchin' Kitchen, *Vegan Food & Living* magazine, PETA.org and more.

Index